The Gamekeeper at Home ... and Abroad

A Sporting Life in Britain and France

J C Jeremy Hobson

skycat
publications
www.skycatpublications.com

Published in 2014 by Skycat Publications
Vaiseys Farm, Brent Eleigh, Suffolk CO10 9PA
Email info@skycatpublications.com
www.skycatpublications.com

ISBN 978 0 9927451 7 2

Printed by Latimer Trend & Company Ltd
Estover Road, Plymouth, Devon PL6 7PY United Kingdom
Tel: 01752 201930 Fax: 01752 201760
Email: Sales@latimertrend.co.uk
www.latimertrend.co.uk

© 2014 J C Jeremy Hobson

Any description of hunting outside the restrictions of the Hunting Act which came into
force in February 2005 must be understood to have taken place before its inception.

The information contained in this book is true and complete to the best of our
knowledge. All recommendations are made without any guarantee on the part of the
author or publishers, who also disclaim any liability in connection with the use of this
data or specific details.

The source of photographs is credited alongside the image: where there is no credit
shown, these are the author's own.

About the Author

JEREMY HOBSON is a professional freelance writer and author and a member of the Guild of Agricultural Journalists. He is well-known for his countless magazine articles and over 30 published books – the main subject matter of which concerns most aspects of country living. His passion is hunting but his interests range from horse riding to amassing an eclectic collection of rare and second-hand books; and from cookery to poultry keeping.

Jeremy considers himself extremely fortunate that, throughout his life, he has been paid to do what he enjoys most and, since his first published article appeared in 1976 and his first book a decade later, has been a prolific commentator on matters rural.

Other books by J C Jeremy Hobson

Dogs & hunting

Beagling	David & Charles
Working Terriers	Crowood
Gundogs: your problems solved	Batsford
Trail Hunting, Rabbiting and Ratting with Hounds	
and Terriers	Skycat Publications

Shooting & gamekeeping

Small-scale Game Rearing	Crowood
Gamekeeping	Crowood
What Every Gun Should Know	David & Charles
Cultivating a Shoot	David & Charles
Running a Shoot	Crowood
The Shoot Lunch	Quiller
A Practical Guide to Modern Gamekeeping	How To Books
Sporting Lodges: Sanctuaries, Havens & Retreats	Quiller

Smallholdings & livestock

Successful Smallholding (co-authored with Phil Rant)	Crowood
Keeping Pigs (co-authored with Phil Rant)	David & Charles

Poultry & chickens

Bantams: a Guide to Keeping, Breeding and Showing	Crowood
Backyard Poultry Keeping	Crowood
Backyard Ducks and Geese	Crowood
Keeping Chickens (co-authored with Celia Lewis)	David & Charles
Keeping Chickens (2nd, revised, edition)	David & Charles
Choosing and Raising Chickens	David & Charles
Élever des poules	Terres éditions
Success with Chickens	Quiller
Keeping Chickens (3rd, revised, edition)	David & Charles

Country cooking & cookery

Cook Game	Crowood
The New Country Cook	Crowood
Chutneys, Pickles and Relishes	Crowood
The Rabbit Cook	Crowood
The Pigeon Cook	Crowood

Rural living & country interests

Rural Living in France	Survival Books
Curious Country Customs	David & Charles

Miscellaneous

The Lost Poems of W. H. Kennings (ed)	Blackwell Printers

Author's note

IT must be made clear that some of what is recorded here took place before the Hunting Act 2004 and so there may be some practices described which are not nowadays legal as a result. It is as much for this reason as any other that I've included the month and year dates – as one would a diary – as a timeline reference. Also, the laws regarding field sports vary tremendously between Britain and France and what is described as being permissible in one country may not be in the other. In addition, any prices given in the text were correct at the time the piece was originally written.

It is important to note that, wherever possible, I have tried to avoid using inclusive pronouns (e.g. "his or her" and "he and she") in the text: sometimes though, for pure convenience, I have used "he" as a neutral pronoun and absolutely no sexist inference should be taken from this.

Also, unless specifically stated, the reference to any company, organization, product or publication in this book does not constitute an endorsement or recommendation.

Dedication

"A stranger is just a friend I haven't met yet."
Will Rogers: 1879-1935

To all the fieldsports men and women of Britain and France who I've met over the years – and to those whom I've yet to meet.

Acknowledgements

MUCH of what appears in the following pages has previously been published over the last decade in my regular *"Sporting Life from Le Garde de Chasse"* column in *The Countryman's Weekly* and I am most grateful to Tracey Allen and everyone at that particular publication for permission to reproduce it here. Thank you all.

In accordance with my understanding of the UK's copyright laws, in the original articles I did not seek permission to quote minor extracts taken from book, magazine and Internet where they amounted to merely a few words – but can assure anyone concerned that I have never taken any quote and used it out of context … or to the detriment of what was intended by the author. I also, on every occasion, credited the author and identified the publication. However, should anyone reading the following feel that I should have done more, I can only offer my apologies and ask them to contact either myself or the publishers in order that amends can be made in any future reprints.

As far as photographs are concerned, unless there is credit given alongside, it should be assumed they are my own – or that old illustrations are out of copyright.

Contents

Preface

SOME people talk of Fate, others of luck. Yet more speak of "making your own luck" – and I think it's probably the latter school of thought to which I subscribe. I've undoubtedly been "lucky" all my life but much of it has come about as a result of making contacts or being in the right place at the right time.

Had my parents not, for instance, taken my brother and me on holiday in North Yorkshire when I was about eleven, I would not have seen the grouse shooting party going up onto the moors on the "Glorious Twelfth" – and perhaps never had the idea of finding out more and subsequently deciding upon gamekeeping as a career. Interested in poultry from a very early age, it was whilst buying a second-hand chicken ark that the conversation somehow got around to the subject of keepering – and to the seller saying that he knew of a head keeper who was looking for an assistant keeper. Contacts were made and the job provided the perfect experience prior to my attending college in order to study game and sporting management.

Afterwards, a letter sent by me on "spec" to one landowner resulted in a season's work helping out on his grouse moor and then, just when that particular door was due to close, someone I met at college recommended me to a shoot owner in Surrey – where I spent seven happy years before being asked by one of the guest Guns whether I'd be interested in expanding and building up his West Sussex shoot. Twenty years, two children, a second marriage and two step-sons later, circumstances brought about the possibility of a move to France.

Just how "fate" and "luck" take hold of life is further evidenced by how we came to "Le Malineau"; our house in France. Whilst keepering in West Sussex, I used to ride to hounds – and got to know my farrier as much as a friend as for his expertise in keeping my horse shod and on the hunting field (quite difficult in the Wealden clay which pulled shoes off with persistent regularity!). However, eventually deciding he was getting too old for the job, he and his partner moved to France … but we kept in touch. Sadly, Barry died some years later and my wife and I came out to see Jilly. During conversation, she mentioned that, for financial reasons, she had to sell and – to quote the oft-used cliché, "the rest is history".

But fate hadn't finished with us yet! In the two years we'd lived in France the West Sussex shoot had been sold and one Sunday morning, the new owner rang to ask if I would interested in acting as host to the visiting Guns on a shooting day as various business commitments on his part meant that he wouldn't be around – or indeed in the UK – for much of the foreseeable future. So it was that I began a new and totally unexpected seasonal career as a "shoot captain" alongside my precarious full-time freelance writing profession which I had started upon arriving in the French countryside as a means of keeping the proverbial wolf from the door.

I had, though, already been writing regularly for the likes of *Shooting Times*, *Countrysport*, *Gamekeeper & Countryside*, *Farmer's Weekly*, *Fancy Fowl* and *Smallholder* over the many years I'd been working as a keeper. In the late 1980s and early 1990s (again as a result of being in the right place at the right time) I even dipped my toes into the shark-infested waters of the radio and television media; contributing to BBC2's *Tracks* programme, ITV's *Country Ways*, Radio 4's *The Countryside in …* series amongst others. Various commissioned feature pieces included work for *The Field*, *Country Life*, *Horse & Hound*, *Shooting & Conservation*, the Scottish Opera and several regional newspapers. Nowadays, I have my own column in *French Property News*, *Your Chickens* and of course, *Countryman's Weekly* – from the nucleus of which, *The Gamekeeper at Home … and Abroad* has grown.

And just how did I come upon the idea for this particular book title? Well, many will know of the classic, *The Gamekeeper at Home* by Richard Jefferies (first published in 1878 and re-printed countless times since) and it somehow seemed a natural (if possibly cheeky) progression to add to Jefferies' title in order to encompass both my gamekeeping career at home in Britain and my most recent years living in France. In addition, in France, the gamekeeper is generically referred to as "Le Garde Chasse" and this, together with a sub-heading of "a sporting life" has been the name by which my *Countryman's Weekly* column has been known for the past decade.

Jeremy Hobson
"Le Malineau"
Summer 2014

1

A Sporting Life
and Rural Living

W HEN it comes to a sporting life, the French populace is a mass of contradictions, not the least of which is their attitude towards their animals. In spite of what appears to me to be the casual neglect of many sporting dogs throughout the close season, any actual evidence of assault, ill-treatment, abandonment, torture and neglect all constitute mistreatment and, under French law, there are heavy penalties – including fines and imprisonment.

Other apparent contradictions that I've still not managed to get to grips with despite having lived in France for twelve years now, include the fact that it's possible to walk straight into a gun shop and buy a weapon, but to shoot game you must have completed the quite rigorous test that is the "permis de chasse". Of course the purchase of a gun is not quite as simple as I've made out and some form of identification and proof of address is required but it is nevertheless, a far more relaxed operation than in the UK.

In a few parts of the country – mainly the south-east regions – the taking of thrushes, fieldfares and blackbirds is a traditional sport and yet regardless of this fact wild bird numbers remain quite healthy. For a country with an undeserved reputation for killing "anything that moves", why is it then that France has some of the most efficacious and seriously funded conservation groups looking after both the wellbeing of the countryside in general and field sports participants in particular?

The first thing that strikes you when following hounds in France is that it is rare to see hunt staff or the mounted field on anything but an ordinary "nag". Many are, I believe, ex-trotting horses given a new career but generally, the horse is a vehicle on which to hunt rather than riding to hounds being a pleasure in its own right. Times are changing, though, and the popularity of horse and pony riding is ever-increasing – with the result that there are some fantastic looking horses being kept by the "hobbyist". Nonetheless, the fact remains that some 850 horses are still eaten each day by the French.

Even accepting that, apart from the Parisian lady who treats her lap dog like a child, the average French person does not get as attached to their animals, be they pet or farmyard. I would have thought that the idea of paying to watch wild beasts perform their tricks in a tatty tent would not hold much appeal. Unfortunately, it appears that the traveling circus is still a popular spectacle here and, over the years, I've witnessed the sad and somewhat surreal sight of camels, llamas and zebras tethered on roadside verges – and even a trailer of lions parked up in the front of the local bar/tabac. Yet, just up the road from us at Doue la Fontaine there is a zoological

Above: Whilst the British shooter generally prefers a side-by-side ...

*Right:
... typically, the French Gun uses an over and under.*

(Photos: Elliot Hobson)

establishment known world-wide for its various conservation projects – and birds and animals bred there are frequently released back into their natural environment as part of all-important worldwide rehabilitation programmes. Très bizarre!

Fishing in France
23rd March 2006

It has to be said that despite the unrivalled opportunities, the average French angler seems to prefer coarse fishing to game fishing. Coarse fishing is big business and it is not surprising when one considers the fact that seventy-five species of fish live and breed in the lakes, rivers, ponds, reservoirs and canals. A fishing club, private landowner or the local community will probably own the rights to the water and often stretches of a river are divided between local clubs which anglers must join in order to fish there. Signs such as "pêche reserve" or "pêche gardée" are common and denote private fishing.

Waters are split into two – 1st (première) and 2nd (2ème) categories. In the first, you can fish for trout and, in some cases, salmon, but despite only having paid to fish for game, it's possible to fish also for carp, perch, pike and zander on many of these waters. 2nd category waters are for coarse fishing and generally, allow fishing all the year round. Typically for France, nothing is straightforward and there are certain exceptions where a spring close season exists for pike and zander in both 1st and 2nd category waters!

Night fishing areas ("parcours de pêche de nuit") are identified by "lots", which are simply a way of dividing up rivers into manageable sections and are numbered sequentially. Such zones are clearly signposted on the bank-side. When night fishing, or at any other time, for that matter, look out for the government electricity company (EDF) danger signs – "Sous les lignes prudence restons à distance" – and take great care when using rods anywhere near pylons as the introduction of graphite in the manufacture of the continental fishing pole has greatly increased the risk of death by electrocution from contact with overhead power lines.

For the sea fishing enthusiast, boats can be hired from one of the many ports and harbours that organise deep-sea fishing expeditions. Not being much of a sea fisherman myself, I know little about it, but I'm told by those who do that the fishing off the Atlantic coast is better than that to be found around the Mediterranean. Fishing in ports is not permitted but you can fish anywhere else along the sea front. In addition, your catch must be of a certain size in order to spare younger fish and this minimum size varies according to the region. Even though you might see the locals out on the mud flaps and beaches, gathering shellfish is also strictly limited, especially sea urchins and oysters, which are seasonal. To avoid any potential misunderstandings, it's best to visit the local maritime affairs office to find out more.

Very importantly, if you're visiting France on a fishing holiday, it would be a wise move to sterilize your equipment after returning home to the UK and before heading for any British rivers and lakes. Unlike France, Britain is currently free of the Gyrodactylus salis parasite that attacks the skin, fins and gills of salmon, trout and some other freshwater fish. The only means of eradication, were it to affect the UK, would be the complete destruction of whole catchments of fish so cleaning all your gear is obviously a wise precaution.

The pleasures and practicalities of game fishing
20th May 2009

The thousands of miles of river banks here in France make it very easy to find somewhere to fish. There are coarse fishing ponds and lakes in Normandy and icy mountain streams tumbling down the Pyrenees. In the thousands of miles in between you can take your pick almost anywhere.

In the Pyrenees there are the wildest of all wild brown trout and, unlike many other parts of Europe, some exciting bank-side fly fishing can be had relatively cheaply. Other rivers run wide, and sometimes high, requiring what can be at times, some tricky wading (May and June are the times for the "run-off" in these regions). In that part of France, just being there gives as great a pleasure as the fishing itself and, positioned quietly on the banks, it might perhaps be possible to see rare Egyptian vultures currently being released as part of a rehabilitation programme led by our local zoo at Doue le Fontaine here in the western Loire.

Most fishing is controlled by local fishing associations, known as "Associations pour la Pêche et la Protection du Milieu Aquatique"

(APPMA's) and buying a local fishing licence in one area for the season may well also allow you to fish in other regions – in others however, it will be necessary to buy a complementary permit for a few additional euros. As well as a season ticket, some departments of France offer a holiday permit which is valid for two weeks and, since 2007, it has also been possible to purchase day tickets in some, but by no means all, regions. The holiday ticket, a "Carte vacances", does away with the need for membership of one of the APPMA's and also covers the "taxe piscole" – the French equivalent of a national rod licence. Private waters could require the would-be fisherman to purchase a day ticket in addition to the licence.

The dry fly fishing season here begins in March and is a popular pastime from then until the early summer. August can be hot and the fish sluggish, but it's possible that the cooler dawns and dusks of September may rejuvenate them and, as a result, some good days can

Fishing – clothing and equipment may change but the passion remains the same!

be had before the season closes once more on the third weekend of the month. Some regions, however; of which Normandy is one, permits fly fishing to continue until the beginning of October.

No smoke without fire
13th August 2008

Despite having been away from the grouse moors for many years now, I always think of them on the 12th of August. In fact, it was seeing Lord Bolton's shooting party making their way up on to the moors for the opening day of the season way back in 1969 that first gave me the idea of becoming a gamekeeper – a decision that didn't go down very well with my career's master at school who was more used to advising pupils in engineering apprenticeships; university entrance exams and college courses. Nonetheless, and despite his best efforts to thwart my ambitions, I managed over the years, not only to secure some very good lowland employment, but also some very interesting and enjoyable times on the grouse moors of both West and North Yorkshire and it is the memories of these that are evoked each year when the grouse shooting season once again begins.

I cannot ever remember the weather on the "Twelfth" being anything other than sunny and warm – a very different matter to the days at the end of October, or during the keeper's shoots in early December when no shooting coat ever made was sufficient to maintain body heat or repel driving moorland rain. On the opening day though, it was generally shirt-sleeves attire for the beaters and flankers and each step in the long heather would produce a pollen from the bloom so heady that it lingered for weeks on tweed breeches and caused no end of problems as far as the scenting abilities of the dogs were concerned; especially for those picking-up around the butts.

In 1975, however, it wasn't the heather we keepers could smell as dawn broke on opening day, but the pungent aroma of burning peat. I was working for the Earl of Swinton at the time and, a week before, the estate office had been contacted by the local RAF station to inform them that a large part of the heather was on fire. It being an estate totaling some 27,000 acres, not all parts could be seen from the four moor-keeper's cottages and the flames had gone un-noticed until being spotted by a keen-eyed pilot. It was, as Sod's Law would have it, in the most inaccessible place and necessitated the assistance of the army, several local fire engines and also tenant farmers who all met at the nearest possible point before transferring milk churns and tanks full of water onto tractors, trailers and the backs of Land Rovers and getting as close to the front of the fire as possible.

It took two days to completely beat out all the flames that kept re-igniting and, even when the other helpers had gone, it was still necessary for the keepers to spend the following nights sleeping in nearby grouse butts in order to be "on watch", as there was always the danger of the fire continuing to burn under the peat. What a tiring time that particular opening week proved to be – not only had we been sleeping rough, but the way the shooting was planned meant that we were involved in shoot day organization for five days running as well as keeping an eye out for signs of any new fire outbreak.

Sporting "firsts"
18th April 2012

I can vividly recollect the first shooting day for which I was totally responsible as a single-handed gamekeeper – but it was not for any of

A moorland fire can be both spectacular and alarming … and a cause for lack of sleep!

the causes one might suppose. In the exuberance of youth, I'd agreed to go to a party many miles away the evening before and, for long and complicated reasons (which eventually involved a visit to a police station) it seemed that, at 06.00am on the dawn of the shoot, there was no way I could be back at the yard for nine o'clock in order to meet the beaters and Guns. Thankfully I did so – with minutes to spare and having had no sleep at all!

My first day ever riding to foxhounds was on a borrowed mare by the name of "Triffena". I don't remember what sort of day we had but I do recall being absolutely exhausted as a result of her very peculiar and uncomfortable action. The "tri" part of her name was very apt as it seemed, after being in the saddle for a while, that she was operating on three legs rather than four! I do, though, remember both horse and day on my first time out with a pack of French hounds. Whilst not as strange in gait as "Triffena", my mount was an ex-trotter and rather than canter anywhere, was content to travel at a liver-shaking fast pace, as a result of which, it was impossible to ride in the classic English manner. She was also quite small and I had to have my stirrups almost jockey-style so as to prevent my long legs from reaching the ground! However, the pomp and ceremony of all the horn-blowing and the magnificent uniforms of the hunt staff, plus the grandeur of the woods through which we were hunting made it all very memorable indeed.

Whilst we may not remember our first day out with hounds, rod or gun, none of us ever forget those "red-letter days" when we might have been lucky enough to shoot our first woodcock or catch a fish that has been particularly elusive. One personal experience of fly-fishing was actually both a "red letter day" and a "first". After a fruitless evening on the river, a friend and I decided to give it best and go to the pub; as we wandered back along the bank, we noticed a large brown trout on the other side of the water. At first undecided whether or not to bother, I thought it worth an exploratory cast and, very unusually for me, dropped a fly perfectly just up-stream of the fish … as the fly drifted over the trout, it took in text-book fashion and eventually I played it over, and into, the landing net being held by my friend. That, and the pint which followed, was the perfect end to a perfect summer's evening on a southern chalk stream.

Patrice, the icon of Paris fashion!
8th April 2009

Apparently, Patrice, our local game farmer, was involved in this year's Paris Fashion Week held in March. Looking at him, you'd find it difficult to see why – he's certainly not model material and I've never seen him wearing anything remotely fashionable. Unless that is, you include the latest design of off-the-peg camouflage trousers bought for 15 euros at our local supermarket. In actual fact, Patrice's actual one and only connection to this most prestigious of fashion dates is that, back in the autumn, he supplied a well-known designer with a quantity of game bird feathers which were used as adornments to belts and hats but, listening to Patrice in the bar the other evening, you would have been forgiven for thinking that he had single-handedly saved the world's clothing industry with his contribution.

From what I've since read and seen on television, it seems that feathers are the "in thing" on this season's catwalks and that all the best shops in Paris and London are stocking a wide variety of clothes and accessories trimmed with feathers. Now we, as country-people have long seen feathers as a useful by-product of our sport and many of us, should we be lucky enough to shoot one, will place a woodcock's pin feather in our hat-band as a memento of a special day or, if of a more flamboyant, Oscar Wilde type nature, a long curling feather plucked from the tail of a pheasant.

You would think that there can be no harm in using the feathers of shot game or domestic fowl killed for the table in such useful ways and it is, on the face of it, surely to be applauded that we make as much use of every part of the bird as we can. According to the fashion papers, the issue has however, ruffled the feathers of the pro-vegan animal rights group PETA. In true sensationalist style, the organisation is going round the catwalks of Europe and telling anyone who will listen, that there is cruelty involved in the collection of feathers and that "most birds have them painfully ripped off or cut out while they are still alive". Erroneously, or so it would appear, I and many thousands of other country dwellers, thought feathers were simply an incidental by-product of meat production in much the same way as is leather. Having heard PETA's wise words, I cannot now get out of my head the picture of a poor, luckless trout fisherman chasing round an enclosure of farmed ostrich in an attempt to catch and pluck a few specimens with which to create a Marabou-type fly pattern.

Feathers of all kinds are essential to the fly-tier who will, with utmost skill, produce the most realistic imitations from the capes of cock chickens, the hackles of guinea fowl and even the feathers of duck gathered from around the preening gland behind the "parson's nose". Abbreviated to the name of the "C.D.C feather" by British fly-tiers, the French, in their usual manner, give the feathers from this part of the bird the glorious title of "l'Croupion de canard".

Feathers, when you think about it, have been an essential part of country living and sporting life for many centuries. Apart from their obvious use in bedding and clothes – which is strange really, as compared to fur they are relatively inefficient in keeping us warm – and as fishing lures, beauty adornments, writing implements and for religious purposes, they were of course, important as flights for stabilising arrows.

Many of the battles won or lost over the centuries have relied on the success or otherwise of their regiments of archers. Occasionally;

and when I'm feeling brave enough or drunk enough, I will remind the French in our local bar of the English battle successes, especially if they are rubbing my nose in it over the fact that France has pipped at the post a British country at rugby; they are leading in the Tour de France or that a French yachtsman has beaten an English one into second place.

The archers of war-time have given us several sayings and traditions, probably the most famous of which is the universally recognised two-fingered "salute". The expression "a feather in his cap" has its origins on the battlefield, as indeed does the fact that the Prince of Wales' coat of arms has depicted three ostrich plumes ever since the Battle of Crecy in 1346 when Edward, Prince of Wales positioned his knights in the centre of a crescent of 10,000 archers. Much later, a white chicken feather was occasionally sent as an insult and hostile suggestion of cowardice to male recipients who, to the mind of the sender, should have been fighting in the trenches of the First World War rather than being at home. It was in fact, more cowardice on the part of the sender who was almost always anonymous and failed to understand, or take into account that many of these men had been invalided home suffering from shell-shock.

In Native American culture, the feather's of a blue jay were the badge of office of a medicine man and, in February this year, a judge in Salt Lake City, ruled that a federal ban on the possession of eagle feathers by "non-Indians"

Feathers adorn many varieties of hats!

was too restrictive. So, the next time that you pluck a bird and use its plumage for some secondary purpose, remember that feathers have a history and been a part of culture and sporting life for as long as Man has been around and, over that time, used for a multitude of purposes.

RURAL LIVING

There's a lot of countryside in France – and a variety of farming practices to go with it. In many cases the farms and vineyards are run by the sons and daughters of generations who have not moved far from where they were born and it's not unusual for the father or grandfather to be on hand to offer help, advice and criticism in equal measure!

It is a sweeping statement but, in our area nonetheless true, that the French rural elderly are a unique breed. They are stereotypical in that the majority of gents still wear berets and blue denim, and the ladies nylon dresses the like of which was last seen by your grandmother in the 1960s. They are extremely knowledgeable on all matters "country" and, if our experiences are anything to go by, make for very friendly neighbours. The most elderly of them have also been affected by World War Two as, no matter in which part of France they live, they cannot fail but to have been distressed by the German occupation. In our area the Resistance was quite strong and there are several churches whose walls still show signs of machine gun fire where Resistance fighters were lined up and then shot. A salutary reminder of what today's elderly could well have seen in their childhood.

A hole in the ground
20th May 2009

I want to be a French road-mender. Not one of those you pass on the péage whose work is announced kilometres ahead by the huge flashing arrows attached to the back of a works lorry and whom you are exhorted to consider on the LED notifications illuminating overhead gantries, but a real rural road-repair-man with a smile on my face and a shovel to lean on.

Like those in Britain, small sequestered highways in the French countryside suffer during the winter storms, but despite this, I have to say that even the tarmaced track which is commune-owned and goes no

The older generation of Frenchman is not hard to find!

further than our house is in far better state than many of the UK country lanes that carry all manner of daily "rat-run" traffic.

The reason we are so blessed is because there is a "system" (not that I've worked it out yet) whereby every single road, no matter how small, is attended to on an annual basis, and the verges and ditches down each side are cut and dug in the spring and early autumn: as a consequence of which, the rain comes down, the roads get wet, the rain runs off, and the ditches take the surface water as far as the nearest stream. Even the farmers take advantage of the ditches and, after drilling a cereal field, will often bring a single plough furrow through the field's lowest point and directly to the ditch so that rarely does one ever see standing water on the fields, no matter how hard it has rained.

But I digress from my ambition to become a rural road-mender. Let me tell you how it works. Every commune has an "amenities man and van" that keeps the place looking tidy and even decorates the village square with seasonal boughs and decorations at Christmas. In addition, there periodically appears from somewhere – possibly from a subterranean cave where they have been gently slumbering – two ancient dungaree-clad men with wrinkled smiles on their faces and an equally ancient tractor. To the hydraulics of the smoke-belching beast (I'm talking of the machine and not its Gitane-fuelled master) is attached a small metal box, into which has previously been deposited a quantity of tarmac and gravel.

With cheerfulness reminiscent of almost any of the Seven Dwarves, one of the men hauls himself onto the tractor seat and sets forth to do battle. Following behind is the second man, armed with a shovel, a toothless grin and a nut berry-brown complexion. The procession sets off at a gentle walking pace until an uneven piece of road is found; the tractor pulls just past it, the walking attendant scoops his shovel into the box of black magic mending dust and flings a liberal coating into the pot-hole. The tractor then reverses and "steam-rollers" it into a firm surface before the group moves on.

Now, possibly the best thing about it all is that no prior preparation seems to be required; if there are grass and weeds growing around the hole, or through a crack in the surface, it's of no consequence, the plants get covered too.

I suppose no-one is ever as happy as they might outwardly seem, but to me, judging from our particular team of two, it seems an idyllic life – no wonder I have this periodic thought of how wonderful it would be to be ambling along country roads observing nature, taking in the summer sun and occasionally strewing the commune's highways with a shovel or two of tarmac and gravel.

Contemplating a move to France
6th June 20012

I occasionally receive requests for advice regarding property buying in France. Individual requirements obviously differ, but it is surprising just what proportion of people who get in touch have a specific interest in field sports and rural living. For this reason, just in case any readers are contemplating a move to France, I thought a few personal observations might be of interest.

The first worry is, of course, the language. Not many people in rural France speak English; also, French "officialdom" generally necessitates any forms to be completed in triplicate. Even if your circumstances don't change from one year to the next, you'll annually still be expected to provide reams of photocopies to substantiate the details previously provided – it matters not if they contain exactly the same information!

Many come with no real idea as to how they might supplement UK savings or a pension: most naively think that they will run a "gîte" or offer other forms of holiday accommodation and the world will come rushing to their door. Sadly, no matter what part of the country one might be intending to put down roots, there are almost certainly more available holiday lets than there are takers and for this reason it is better not to rely on the tourist trade as a potential income. On the plus side, contrary to what many people will tell you, the income tax expected from an individual is far less than the UK – unless, that is, I've been blessed with a bad accountant and I will, some time in the future, be told that I've been under-paying for the last decade!

Assuming that all is well financially, the next "problem" is likely to be where exactly one should decide to live. France is such a big country! Many people choose Brittany, Normandy, or any of the northern regions purely and simply because of the close proximity to ferry ports and Britain. If, however, you want to be in a part of France that really feels like France, you need to consider south of the Loire. Individual departments are known to be graded as far as being the cheapest (or most expensive!) to live. "Le Malineau" is just on the border of Deux Sevres and the Maine-et-Loire: fortunately, being on the right side of the border (Deux Sevres), we pay far less in the way of community charges. If we didn't live where we do, the Limousin would be my next choice as far as the cost of living is concerned – and also for its beauty. It does though, have its own micro-climate and several times I've driven through the more northern parts in August when the grass has been dry, parched and brown at home but remains green and verdant on the pastures there.

Sporting-wise, almost every region has its opportunities. There are plenty of rivers and lakes for fishing and, in most cases, it ought to be possible to take part in some commune rough-shooting once one has obtained the "permis de chasse", taken out insurance and joined a local group of like-minded individuals. Clay shooting events are a very popular summer pastime throughout France … but again, it pays to join a club, of which there are many.

Contemplating a move to France?

If hunting with hounds is important, it all depends on what particular aspect you are most interested. There are, after all, regions where underground terrier work is popular (and legal) and others where "rabbit packs" of beagles abound – which are obviously perfect for the foot-follower. But, such is the nature of hunting in heavily-wooded areas, foot followers are as likely to see as much of the sport when it comes to boar and deer hunting as will the mounted field. My advice would be to find an area in which you might be interested and then take a summer holiday at a time when there is a "fête de la chasse" in the locality. There are bound to be plenty of hounds and terriers on display, the masters of which will be only too happy to tell you more.

It must be said that moving to France is not always the idyllic dream most people expect. It can cause tension amongst a family and if you have children of school age, it is important to consider exactly what age they are. From the experience of others, it seems that primary school children adapt very quickly but early teenagers find it more difficult to drop into the French schooling system. By far the most common problem though, is when one of an adult couple is less keen on the move than the other. It has to be said that the majority of men adapt wonderfully to their new life; their female partners less so … as can be evidenced from several "expats" of my acquaintance where sadly, a relationship has broken up as a result. The two main reasons given are, missing the family "back home" and a lack of understanding the language.

Less importantly, but a factor to consider nonetheless, is the subject of buying a property with a lot of land. In theory, the idea is wonderful and, it being far more affordable than in the UK, the prospect of all-inclusive fields and woodland is a dream to which we all aspire. The practicalities of managing it can, however, be another matter entirely and possibly be that one step too far – especially if it is your intention to be only here on a part-time basis.

To earth with a bump
23rd March 2011

I think that, after a lifetime of loving them, I've gone off horses. In fact, I have, quite literally, just gone off a horse and I write this with a bruised shoulder and a hoof print in my chest!

A few years ago, I used to ride a neighbour's horse with weekly regularity. Sadly, the animal was subsequently sold and exactly how long ago it was that I last rode here in France was brought home to me when I recently up-ended my riding boots and found a mummified lizard – quite how it got in there is open to speculation! It is, I think, a general countryman's trick to up-end any pair of boots or shoes that hasn't been worn for a long time because, sure as eggs are eggs, something not too pleasant will have taken up residence. The fact that such footwear is usually kept in an out-house or utility room does not help and I'm sure that most of us, will, at some stage in our sporting career, have found spiders, mice and a whole host of other creatures living a rent-free life. But I digress and the reason that I was donning my riding boots was because of a kind offer to ride a newly acquired horse from the Cadre Noir, a cavalry establishment located at nearby Saumur.

The Cadre Noir is, like the Viennese Riding School, world famous for its equitation and demonstrations both here and abroad and, having watched them execute their skills on their home ground at Saumur, it is, most definitely an event not to be missed. Part of their routine is to carry out a combined "hop-skip-and-a-jump" whilst the horse is rearing on its back legs. It is, apparently, a war move dating back several centuries and was taught to all cavalrymen in order that they could avoid the sword-slashing of foot-soldiers. Having seen the top performers carry out this act, I have always been of the opinion that it is un-natural and cruel. My recent experience tells me that, once learnt, their animals never forget!

Tacked up and ready to go, my 17 hands war-fighting machine was a placid as a seaside donkey. However, once he realised that he was going out on his own and not performing in company with his equine mates, it was a totally different scenario: he napped, whinnied and did all he could to get back to the stable. I nevertheless managed to get him into a quiet walk and then, a quite refined trot. I did, however, baulk at the prospect of taking him over a nearby Roman bridge, thinking that if he suddenly decided to play up, both he and I would be over the low parapet and into the river running below.

Relatively relaxed, I began to enjoy the ride until, most unexpectedly, he decided that enough was enough and performed possibly the most exquisite "courbette" ever seen. Sadly, despite managing to maintain my seat during the initial rearing, I was taken unawares by his ensuing prancing and was, at the end of it all, on the ground in a crumpled heap. At least he didn't run off and I did, as they say you should, get straight back on after having first conversed with him in fluent Anglo-Saxon!

Lost in the language
11th March 2012

After almost a decade living here in France, there are still many aspects of day-to-day conversation with our neighbours where I lose the thread entirely, or manage to catch up just as the subject matter moves elsewhere. Nowhere does this happen more often than when discussing things of a field sports nature, or when talking of our various sporting lives, especially when it happens to be in the company of some of Maurice's shooting cronies who complicate matters further by speaking in the local "patois" or dialect.

Fortunately, I manage to pick up on some of what is being said because of the fact that many French words have, over many generations, been incorporated into British sporting life. Most of these appertain to hunting language. When, for example, anyone talks of "renard" over here, it takes no thinking at all to immediately know that they mean a fox purely because, in Britain, "Reynard" has been used as a colloquial name for the huntsman's quarry and the gamekeeper's nightmare ever since the days of William the Conqueror.

There are plenty of modern day French words that occur in UK deerstalking – the most obvious being "venaison" and venison. Some are, however, more easily worked out than others; the French word for throat is "gorge" and the part of a deer under its throat is known as "gorget" on both sides of the Channel.

Because I've long had an interest in collecting any old books concerning fieldsports, especially those from the Edwardian period, I wasn't at all fazed when a Frenchman talked to me about the "battue" as it is a word often used by long-gone English writers to describe the point in a driven game shoot when vast numbers of birds fly fast and furious. When pronouncing it in French, though, it's important to do so correctly as otherwise it can sound like "bateau", their word for "boat", as a result of which, all manner of complications could ensue!

In French, a pair of binoculars is called "jumelles" ... and the male singular of a twin is "jumelle". No wonder I get confused with the language! Photo: Greg Knight (www.ruralshots.com)

I've made many linguistic mistakes since being here. I once told a lady that I'd been married twice and wondered why her face registered a mixture of shock and admiration ... it turns out that what I'd actually said was that I had two wives. Likewise, when informing one of Maurice's shooting friends that my step-sons are twins ("jumeau"), I actually told him that they were a pair of binoculars ("jumelles"). I wasn't too far out with that one however, because the male singular of a twin is "jumelle" – unlike the time my pronunciation was so bad that, whilst I thought I'd casually mentioned to a neighbour that we'd got mice ("souris") in the house, the way I'd spoken seemed to imply that "Le Malineau" was currently full of cherries ("cerise").

Uphill and down dale
27th May 2009

Oh dear. I think I might just have become a mountain biker! Previously I've never had much time or understanding for those mad souls whose idea of fun is to career along woodland paths; the only apparent purpose being to get both them and their bikes as dirty as possible. Any leisure cycling I've been doing here in France has been on the racing bike which I used for training prior to travelling across Mexico with my son ten years ago. The roads around "Le Malineau" are perfect cycle routes; undulating without being hilly and even the most rural are well surfaced and pot-hole free. There's no traffic to speak of either and, if you take steps to avoid the rush hour (the school bus at 07.45am to be precise) you should be OK for at least an hour before running the risk of meeting the travelling bread van coming the other way.

The other Sunday, keen for a bit of exercise before getting down to work on the keyboard, I went out to the shed only to discover that my trusty, rusty steed had a flat tyre. Half awake (it was only 05.30), I couldn't be bothered to make amends and so instead pulled out one of the mountain bikes originally acquired for the use of paying guests in the days when we ran a "gîte" here at "Le Malineau". Fortunately, it had had an outing not that long ago as a result of my daughter and her family being out to see us and its tyres had remained pumped full of air.

On the road and just after calling out "Bonjour Madame Vache" to a friendly-looking house cow (I find it best to keep in with the neighbours), I remembered an interesting track I'd always meant to explore whilst out with the dog but never had. Deviating from my intended route, I was soon pedalling off-road between vines and pasture. Gradually the track got worse and, slipping down a gear or two, I have to confess that it wasn't very long before I was actively seeking out rather than avoiding bumps and dips created by dried out puddles; ducking my head as branches flicked my ears and weaving in and out of trees as if I were an Olympic ski champion negotiating slalom poles.

This mountain bike lark is not as easy as it looks. To maintain momentum in a muddy morass is quite an art and one particular misjudgment in a stretch of dark, sunless woodland led me to end up inspecting France's rural flora at a much closer level than I would have ideally liked. Still, my mishap obviously offered some amusement to a Hoopoe bird which flew off uttering a soft, resonant "ha-ha-ha".

Eventually, faced with the choice of either continuing cross country for more of the same or rejoining the tarmac road, I chose the former option. And do you know what? When I'd reached the end of that track, I went back and (with the exception of ending up in the mud for a second time) did it all again!

2

Hunting with Hounds

PERHAPS the biggest difference between hunting in France and Britain is the topography. Whereas most of the "best" hunting in the UK is carried out over open fields and meadows with hedges, the majority of French hunting is conducted within the confines of the many hectares of huge forests dotted around the country – access to which is obtained by licence. Although many of the packs hunt rabbit, hare, boar, roe deer and occasionally fox, it is stag hunting that is possibly the most popular amongst French hunting folk.

Mounted followers are primarily interested in watching the hounds working and, as is often mentioned by French enthusiasts, "In other countries, people hunt in order to ride, in France we ride in order to hunt!" In practice this can be quite difficult, as the visual restrictions of the woodland, together with the fact that in some forests only the hunt staff are allowed access, means that one has to be very "hound-minded" in order to anticipate where the best view might be had.

Maybe it is this single-mindedness that causes the average mounted supporter to worry less about their personal appearance and also that of their horse. Although at first glance, the general overall turn-out is quite striking, especially when one sees the hunt staff carrying their curled hunting horns across their shoulders; on closer inspection, many participants look as if they might be wearing their grandfather's coat

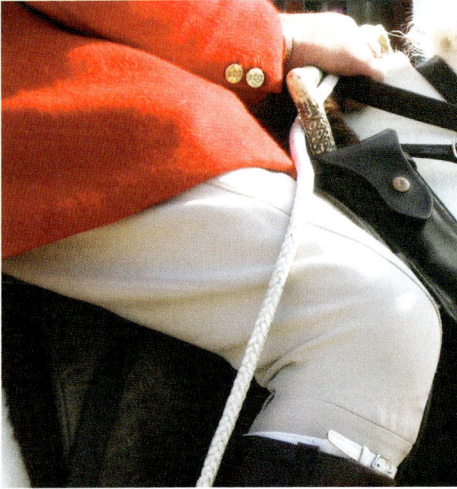

Hunt buttons are also worn on the cuffs of British huntsmen.

that hasn't been brushed since the day it was made. Boots are often dull and even at the meet, be bespattered with mud.

I might be doing grooms and owners a great disservice, but it seems that, unlike our British packs where the huntsman and whippers-in ride some fantastic looking specimens, most of the horses seen out with hounds are quite small and narrow. Many are actually retired trotting horses as the sport is very popular in France and, judging from the adverts in the papers, there are plenty of cheap ones available once their days on the track are over.

As in the UK, each hunt has its own button, but unlike the British packs, everyone wears a stock pin onto which the hunt button has been mounted. Also unlike the UK, where only the hunt staff wears a stock pin in the vertical position, from casual observation, it seems the practice for all subscribers to wear them in this fashion. As to who is what out on the hunting field; it is generally accepted practice that full members and staff are entitled to wear a coloured coat with contrasting velvet cuffs, while all others wear black – as is the case in Britain.

The horn of plenty
28th January 2009

The French hunting horn is, as most people know, not at all like the small, discreet instrument carried by hunts staff in Britain and is instead, a huge curled affair, apparently containing more than four metres of brass tubing. Although at first glance such a horn looks as if it hasn't altered at all since before the Revolution of the late 1700s there is, however, a subtle difference in that back in the days of Louis XIV hunting horns were made to play in a different key. Nowadays, although the shape of the horn hasn't changed in the intervening years, the tone is always in the key of "D". Who, or what, brought about the change is not known, but the fact remains that, even in this modern age, the hunting horn on both sides of the channel is an important part of communications between the huntsman, hounds and the following field.

I say that it is important to the field members, but, in reality, less and less of them seem to understand what the various calls mean and that is a great shame as a great deal of the day's enjoyment is lost by not being able to decipher the sometimes haunting messages being sent through thick woodland or across open fields. When I first became seriously interested in hunting during my early teens, I made every effort to make sense of all the calls; whether it was "Gone away", "Gone to ground and need a terrier", or simply "Going home" but I was, I must admit, very lucky in having a family friend who was the huntsman to the local hounds and who was very patient in blowing the various calls on my behalf – and what is more, blowing them so often, that by the time he'd finished, only an idiot could have failed to recognize each and every one of them.

Of course some huntsmen are better horn blowers than others: there are those who can turn it into such an art form that it makes every hair on the back of your neck stand on end and there are others who make such an appalling noise that their efforts sound like a cow giving birth. In between, there are those who use it purely and simply as the briefest of communications and once that has been done, the horn is slipped back into its pocket until the next time it is needed.

To hear the best of horn blowing in the UK, one either needs to go to a Hunt Ball where a horn-blowing competition is always held, or to a summer hunt-organised event where similar competitions are sometimes held. To hear the best in France, however, one need go no further than on of the many "fête de la chasse" where the horn-blowing competitions are an important feature of the day's happenings. To whet your appetite, listen to some French hunting calls on the Internet by typing "Trompes

Some 4.5 metres of metal are involved in the creation of a French hunting horn!

de chasse St-Hubert" into your search engine and clicking on any one of the many examples to be found on the screen.

T'was the sound of his horn ...
17th October 2012

There is something unbelievably exciting about the sound of a hunting horn in the distance. At the end of last week, I was hanging out the washing and, as I did so, heard either huntsman or master (in France, they are usually one and the same) blowing and calling for some obviously errant hounds. Whilst there was "work in progress" on the computer screen, I had nothing all that urgent vying for my attention and so jumped into the car in order to see if I could find them and watch what was going on.

In doing so, I suppose I was not that much different to those in the past, who, according to the chorus of the song "D'ye ken John Peel", opined that "t'was the sound of his horn brought me from my bed/And the cry of his hounds that he oft times led ..." In that particular situation, and at the time of which was written, it was not, however, lost hounds for whom Peel was blowing, but more that he was gathering hounds together for the start of a day's sport.

In the Lake District, many of the fell packs were made up of individual hounds, all of which were owned and kennelled separately by local farmers and shepherds. On a hunting morning, the huntsman would walk to a setting-off point whilst all the time calling up "his" hounds from all the nearby farms and steadings. Then, after sport had finished, the pack would disband and its members find their own way home again. It must have been fascinating to watch.

Known as "trencher" or "trencher-fed" packs, such goings on were not confined to the Lakeland fells and, in parts of West Yorkshire at the turn of the last century, several harrier packs were kept in the same way. When the horn of their huntsman was heard in the valley, not only would all the farmers, shepherds and other agricultural workers turn out to enjoy the sport, but so too would the weavers and employees of the nearby woolen mills. Fortunately, a great many of the mill owners were keen on their hunting and were ready and willing to spare their workers a half day to follow hounds: although perhaps it was more a case of knowing that, even if they hadn't given their blessing, there were enough workers keen enough on hunting to stage a mass walk-out for the time that the hunt was in the area!

Sometimes blowing a hunting horn at the wrong time could get you into trouble. According to a wonderful book produced by The Holme Valley Beagles in 1986, it seems that, back in 1890, seven local men had been charged with being on licensed premises after the legally permitted time. It was further claimed that they had been singing and blowing a hunting horn at 11.35pm and the police alleged that there "had been several complaints about this being carried on whenever the hounds went in that direction." The men were found guilty and each fined 5s (25p). However, perhaps the main point of interest in this statement is the variety of occupations of the accused as given to the Court. These apparently included three quarrymen, a labourer, a blacksmith, a joiner, a publican and two gamekeepers!

Booted and spurred
17th October 2005

One thing to be noticed when following the French packs of hounds (and also when horn blowing teams are fully kitted out at the summer "fêtes") is the hunting boot. Unlike the traditional British hunting footwear which is, I believe, a descendant of the ones worn by Regency gentlemen who turned the tops of their ordinary boots over when hunting, thereby showing the boot's inner lining (and eventually gave rise to the mahogany tops of a bespoke hunting boot) the French boot is far more flamboyant in that it resembles that of a swashbuckling musketeer. Presumably, the idea is that the extended tops are meant to protect the rider's knees from being damaged by undergrowth as he dashes at full gallop through the woods but, to me, they look very cumbersome and restricting. Traditionally made from the best quality calf leather, today's French hunting boot is however, more likely to be made of natural rubber, which, or so claim the makers of the famous "Venerie" type, is "unmatched for elasticity, suppleness and longevity". Further complimented by a leather lining, it can be customised for height, thereby ensuring that the tops fit perfectly around the individual's knee area.

Although many of us settle for rubber boots when hunting in Britain (some of which are, it must be admitted, indistinguishable from leather), there are still those who, if they can afford it, insist on their boots being made-to-measure. A century ago London used to be able to boast of over 300 boot-makers, but in 2005, there are probably not even ten. Fortunately more still trade in other areas of Britain and in Northamptonshire, the traditional home of boot and shoe manufacturers, can be found Horace Batten, a family firm who have been making riding and hunting boots for seven generations whilst in Wales, the company of Davies Riding Boots supply many hunt servants with made-to-measure boots from their premises in an industrial estate in Gwent.

Followers of French hounds may, or may not, be equipped with spurs and it certainly is not considered essential. In the UK, however, most, if not all regular followers will wear them. To be correct, they must be only worn with the points facing downwards, and then only with "top" or "butcher" boots: butcher boots being plain black without the aforementioned mahogany "tops" and top boots only ever being worn with a hunt coat.

A French hunting boot is raised at the front in order to protect the wearer's knee; a typical British hunting boot has a "mahogany" top.

The earliest spurs were made of wood or bone and they have developed throughout centuries. At first, they were a simple device to goad horses into action, but then became a symbol of rank and chivalry; the best being made of either silver or gold. "Rowels" originated in France in the 1100's and were first recorded in Britain in the 13th Century. Today's hunting spurs are devoid of "rowels" and are mainly made of brass alloy. They are also part of tradition rather than serving any useful purpose, as I have yet to ride a horse that, although it may be sluggish whilst out on a hack or on exercise, does not want to go forward when hounds are in chase!

Hunting side-saddle
14th February 2007

Although I've spent many enjoyable days following hounds in Britain and France, it is nowadays very rare to see any ladies riding side-saddle, which is a great shame as they look so elegant. In my grandmother's era – and I blame both she and my grandfather for my obsession with hunting, shooting and all things country-orientated – it was customary in England for women to ride side-saddle if they hunted and it was considered "indecent" for ladies to ride astride. According to her (she died in the early 1970s aged 96, so her experiences included those from the turn of the century), if one had been taught from an early age to ride side-saddle, the art of riding at speed and jumping wasn't too difficult. I remember her telling me that for hunting, particularly sturdy side-saddles were used, which apparently helped keep the female hunter mounted, but unfortunately had the very serious drawback of sometimes causing injury if the rider fell.

In the 1870s and 1880s, it was unusual for women to ride at speed in order to keep up with a hunting pack; the majority following sedately at a discreet distance and spending much time "coffee-housing" at the covert-side. Eventually, however, some of the more adventurous and "flighty" of them broke ranks with the others and, in order to be able to "ride to hunt" rather than just to be seen, began sitting astride and using an ordinary saddle; no doubt causing much dismay and consternation amongst the "establishment".

Side-saddle; very definitely elegant and feminine!

One groom or two!?
15th June 2011

Yesterday I drove past the farm of someone who I know is a French master of hounds and saw his horses looking in pristine condition in their paddocks. Their summer coat was as fine and polished as a racehorse at its peak and the ends of their tails had been recently cut in "bang" formation so I know they must be regularly cared for – presumably by a professional groom. I say "presumably" but I do not know for certain. Perhaps the M. H. in question dealt with them himself as, no matter whether in France or Britain, times are hard and most people do not nowadays have the luxury of permanent outdoor staff – unlike a century or so ago when it would have been unthinkable to have had to deal with the trivialities and incidentals of one's chosen sport.

In *Notes for Hunting Men* published in 1902, the author was of the opinion "even if a stable only consists of two horses, you must have a man in charge" and that, "for a stud of six horses, a good working head man, a second horseman, and one helper, ought to do; but, if you are hunting often, which means the second horseman is away most of the day, they will have their work cut out to turn horses and saddlery out really well."

Labour might well have been cheap but even so, the number of stable staff recommended does seem a little excessive. It makes you wonder how we all manage the daily minutiae of our chosen field sport in these straightened times!

A Northern sing-song
9th March 2014

Sometimes, in a bar in France, there's an occasional impromptu "sing-song" from the locals – and not usually as a result of the amount of wine that's been drunk, but more for the fun of enjoying and keeping alive a few traditional songs. Parts of Wales has this tradition and, at least when I lived there many moons ago, so too did our part of West Yorkshire, particularly when it came to the singing of hunting songs.

Followers and subscribers of the local packs of beagles and fell-hounds would occasionally organise a "pie and pea" supper and these would always end up with several of those present standing to sing their party-piece. For an outwardly looking rough bunch, there were some surprisingly good voices and many were way better than I've heard since on television's "X Factor" and similar programmes!

Several of those I attended as a teenager were held at the Fleece Inn, at Holme, near Holmfirth and, back in 1987, many of the hunting regulars gathered there in order to record a tape, *Traditional Songs from Summer Wine Country*, which was subsequently sold in aid of a local charity. Many of the songs that were recorded have been passed down by generations via the very strong hunting and shepherding presence in the area; and have been sung regularly at social gatherings throughout the year.

On the recording, Ken Green, one-time huntsman of the Colne Valley, sang "his" song, *The Greetland Hare;* the Holme Valley's huntsman Barry Bridgewater, *The Mardale Hunt;* and Andrew Rogers of the Pennine, regaled the company with *Lakeland, My Beautiful Lakeland* as well as *Drink, Puppy Drink.* I still listen to the tape on occasion as it reminds me of those instrumental in fuelling my youthful enthusiasm for hounds, terriers and all things hunting. However, now 27 years old, the tape cannot go on for much longer and I really must try and find someone with the knowledge, ability and equipment to somehow transfer its contents to CD.

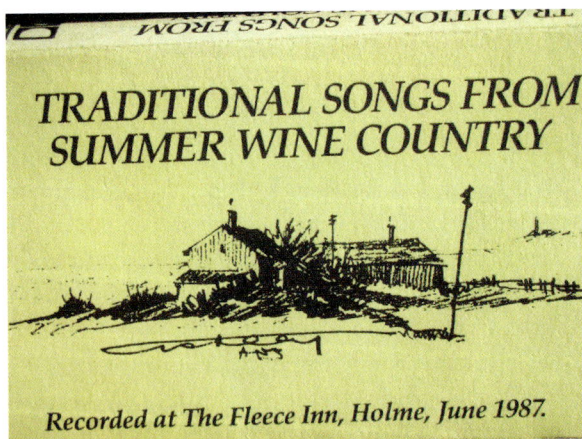

Northern "sing-songs" were recorded for posterity at the Fleece Inn, Holme.

More cunning the fox, the better the sport
23rd August 2009

Before the 2004 Hunting Act, there had always been much discussion in the hunting world about whether or not a hunted fox would deliberately put up a fresh animal so that the hounds would continue on that one's scent rather than follow on the heels of their original quarry. In the early 1940s, there was a BBC radio programme called _Country Magazine_ and I've recently acquired some transcripts, one of which included the words of Dan Evans who told the tale of a hunted fox pushing out a fresh one in front of hounds one day in Monmouthshire.

"The Monmouth foxes are as cunning as they make them, but the more cunning the fox, the better the sport. Many a time I have seen a tired fox enter a covert, "wind" another fox kennelled there and try and switch the chase over to him. I well remember one incident ten or twelve years ago when I was out with the Pentyrch. There was a very useful scent and the hounds put up a vixen on Caerphilly Mountain. A very good hunt followed and the fox ran almost into Roath Park, Cardiff. But there she turned and made for Cefn Mably Wood. The scent was now breast high and the hounds were running at great pace with grand cry.

I was standing just at the edge of one of those beautifully kept rides, out of sight and at the bottom of a dingle; there was a little prill of water at my feet. I felt that the vixen must be tiring rapidly and, unless she could effect a change, would probably be caught. Presently, sure enough, I saw the fox coming down the ride. But this was a great upstanding dog-fox, fresh as paint. Some little distance from him followed the hunted vixen. She came to the little streamlet, and turned up its course, passing very close to me.

The hounds were now very near and she stood frozen to stone within a few yards of me. On came the hounds, simply racing down. They made not the slightest check at the stream but hurried on after the fresh fox. I turned my head and there was the vixen still standing like a statue. Then just as soon as she was sure that the cry of hounds was no longer for her, she gave me a glance and crawled away into deeper brushwood for a well-earned rest."

Clever as it seems to human minds, I doubt whether there can be any premeditation on the part of the hunted fox and it is more likely that it is coincidence when a tired fox runs into a fresh one. The more tired a fox becomes, the less scent he gives off and so it is obvious that hounds will more easily pick up the trail of a fresh animal which has just been roused, and that is presumably what happened in the incident Dan Evans witnessed all those years ago. It used to happen too when a fox took to a drain and found another fox there. When the terriers were entered it was the fresh fox which was more likely to bolt, leaving the hunted fox behind, so hounds would often roll the wrong fox over, the hunt staff never realising that the original animal had lived to run another day.

As well as tiredness, there are other occasions when a fox might not give off much of a smell and many a huntsman has noticed that it was quite common for hounds to draw over a fox without finding him. It appears likely therefore that a fox gives off very little scent when he is lying still. There are other natural defence mechanisms and, as Willy Poole noted in his book *Hunting* (David & Charles 1988), a vixen heavy with cubs usually has very little scent; yet by some perverse twist, a milking vixen often has a strong scent. A fox's scent is also affected by diet and it is reckoned that it will smell differently depending on what it has been eating. Town foxes that scavenge around dustbins give off far less scent than those which are picking up plenty of rabbits, for example.

Very often one smells the rank and unmistakable scent of fox whilst out on an early morning walk or when seeing to the pheasants in the release pens. This does not necessarily mean that he has passed that way just a few minutes ago; indeed it is far more likely that a dog fox has been marking out the limits of his own particular territory sometime during the previous night. The 10th Duke of Beaufort reckoned that to smell such a scent on the morning of a hunting day was a poor omen for it generally meant that the scent was rising and evaporating quickly and as a consequence, it would be a bad day's sport. But, despite the volumes written on the subject of scent by acknowledged hunting experts such as the Duke of Beaufort, Peter Beckford and Tom Smith, despite scientific research, even in the 21st century the whole thing continues to be something of a mystery.

A fine example of the taxidermists' art – but are the adults in this tableau male or female? (See "Sexing a fox")

However, one thing that all agree on is the fact that hounds need to be allowed time to work out a difficult scent. As the famous beagling (and slightly eccentric) fanatic, Jack Ivester Lloyd, once remarked: "The more I see of hunting, the more do I agree with the old huntsman's slogan "leave 'em alone". In other words let them work it out for themselves. They know more about the game than you ever will. Your part in the sport is to stand still and enjoy it, "hollering" them on only to what you are quite certain is the hunted quarry when they have completely lost it."

Sexing a fox
21st April 2010

How often do we all say when retelling the circumstances of the viewing of a fox to a fellow sportsperson, "Oh, he was a big old dog fox with a white tip top his brush"? In actual fact, a difference between the sexes is not always easy to define and, weight-wise at least, there is probably less than two or three pounds between them. Perhaps the illusion of one particular fox being larger than another can be explained by the surroundings in which you see it. Skulking along the bottom of a tall hedgerow it will look small, while if it is encountered in the open and silhouetted against the skyline, a fox of whichever sex will most likely look bigger.

Where obvious differences become more apparent are when comparing the lowland foxes to those that range on the mountains and fells: the latter being generally larger, and certainly longer in the leg. But even so, a difference between the dog and vixen is not often immediately obvious. If you talk to the older generation of moorland keepers or past followers of the fell packs, it is quite likely that they will tell you of the "greyhound" foxes that featured in their parent's and grandparent's sport a hundred years or so ago. They were apparently wilder, greyer and even longer in the leg and muzzle than today's hill foxes and, although I cannot remember for the life of me where I saw it, I did actually once see a mask of such a beast mounted on the wall of a Lake District pub – I wonder if it is still there?

"Greyhound" foxes were certainly known in John Peel's time as evidenced by the fact that a Cumbrian contemporary of Peel's was of the opinion that such a beast could run "aw day and aw through neet, and best part of the next day an' aw." Although comparatively scarce, such foxes would, according to records of the time, sometimes take hounds distances of 50, 60 or even 70 miles.

Moorland foxes can be darker and greyer in colour than their lowground counterparts and on heathland you may find that some foxes there are sandier in colour than those found in heavily wooded areas. As to the famous white tip, I'm not sure that its presence has any bearing at all on what sex of animal to which it is attached, nor to what part of the British countryside a fox is found.

Fred Carno's army!
7th March 2012

This coming Saturday, if all follows as in previous years, there will be hounds in the wood next to "Le Malineau". They are about the same height as an English foxhound and most have that distinctive black, tan and white colouring. If you look closer though, they have a more domed head, slightly deeper rib cage and not as any way near as straight a stern or tail.

They belong to our local gun pack and twice a season they visit in search of any foxes that may be lying up in the wood. This is about the only time that our resident population gets culled as there's not much night shooting of foxes done in our area of France any more. Maurice, our infamous shooting neighbour, does however; remember the times in the mid 1970s when there was an all-out effort to reduce the fox population. Aided by government-funded financial support and bounties, together with earth gassing and night shooting, the offensive was carried out in an effort to eradicate the threat of rabies which had spread firstly from Germany in 1968 and then from Switzerland a short while later.

Thankfully, rabies is almost a thing of the past, due in no small part to the efforts of all those who helped control the foxes almost 40 years ago. It is actually nowadays quite rare to see a fox over here – unlike the part of England where I stay for most of the game shooting season when it is nothing unusual to see one cross a road whilst out and about at night. They are also occasionally seen running from the woods or cover crops during a shooting day, especially in late December and early January when the dogs are searching for vixens in heat.

Be that as it may, if all goes as it has in previous years, Saturday morning will see a white van park at the top of our lane and out will tumble seven or eight couple of hounds. An assortment of other vehicles generally carries the standing Guns who quietly position themselves in our field in readiness for anything that may be flushed from the wood.

In previous years I've had great entertainment watching them from my study window as their attempts can resemble something like Fred Carno's army. On one notable occasion back in 2007, hounds found a fox which then ran into our garden and took temporary refuge under one of our cars before disappearing through the hedge and down a nearby ditch. Hounds followed and some of the Guns ran after them in hot pursuit whilst others dashed to their cars and drove to where the ditch runs parallel to the road in the hope of getting there before the fox. It seemed that they were unsuccessful as, later in the day, I saw the fox wander unconcernedly back through the garden towards the cover from which it was so unceremoniously flushed that same morning!

A balanced view
30th April 2014

Whilst it's reckoned that some 80% of British vets are small animal practitioners, there are others who are extremely knowledgeable of wildlife – and their expert opinions are often sought when any type of research is being carried out into the health and welfare of wildlife.

The Veterinary Association for Wildlife Management (VAWM) has some 570 supporters, most of whom are general veterinary practitioners with clinical experience on all common species of domestic and wild animals.

The objectives of the Association are "to promote the sensible management of British wildlife by methods that are advantageous for the welfare of wild animals and which promote or sustain the health and vigour of their species".

To this end, many of its members are supportive of potentially controversial issues such as hunting with hounds and hare-shooting – as can be evidenced by these quotes from their excellent website:

"Hunting uniquely reproduces the natural selection process whereby weak and sick animals are culled in direct relation to their debility, thereby promoting the health and vigour of the species. Hunting leaves no wounded or damaged survivors ... [it] performs a vital search and dispatch function whereby the weak, the sick and the injured are discovered and quickly dispatched. No other method of culling performs this function and now that hunting is banned, the welfare situation for all hunted species is already worsening."

As far as hare shooting is concerned, the VAWM have this to say:

"Shooting is necessary to control the damage caused to crops and forestry by excessive numbers of hares but it carries the substantial welfare problem of wounding. Up to 25% of hares may not be killed outright by shotguns on hare shoots, half of which may not be recovered even when well trained retrievers are used. Hunting with hounds (beagles, bassets, and harriers) therefore provides an essential search and dispatch system for retrieving wounded animals following hare shoots. It also detects and dispatches other weak and diseased animals in direct relation to their degree of debility thereby helping to maintain the health and vigour of the population as a whole."

What I particularly like, and one with which I whole-heartedly concur, is their opinion that a "balanced wild life population will not result from a 'hands off' approach. In the man-made countryside, control of an over-successful species is best achieved by a combination of legal methods undertaken by farmers, gamekeepers, landowners, naturalists and huntsmen, with their divergent interests using the appropriate methods of control for their particular circumstances."

3

On and Off the Shooting Field

THE strange system of commune shooting that takes place throughout France is, as with most things here, a result of post-Revolution law-making giving the majority equal opportunities – whereas prior to the revolution, such benefits as hunting and the like were the prerogative of the fortunate and wealthy few.

With the exceptions of a few large private shoots run in much the same way as traditional UK estates, shooting is generally organized by municipal associations that, irrespective of who actually owns the land, retain the rights to shoot over all land contained within the municipality – exceptions being where a block of land exceeding 50 hectares comes under single ownership, in which case the landowner can either register his property as a private shoot or let it out to individuals and/or the local shooting association.

The French sporting shooter has had to be equipped with one form of licence or another ever since 1844 when a permit to shoot game was first required. Various licences followed until, in 1974, the "permis de chasseur" was introduced. The theoretical examination was added in July 1976 and then, in 1989, the practical exam became obligatory. In 2013, plans were made to change some of the exam procedures and it was intended that these changes would be operational by January 2014. This being France, they weren't! Originally the responsibility of the "prefecture" of whichever department one happened to be applying, the logistics of the permis de chasseur are nowadays overseen by the Office National de la Chasse et de la Faune Sauvage (l'ONCEF).

Dangerous liaisons
27th March 2013

I've just been reading a report recently released in conjunction with the "Office National de la Chasse et de la Faune Sauvage" which, if I've translated it properly, says that there have been 379 sporting shooting-related fatal accidents throughout France during the last 15 years. It seems that, out of the 90 plus departments, only five have been totally incident free – one of which was Paris where one wouldn't really expect much sporting shooting to take place! The Hérault and the Var had the equal highest number of fatalities over that period with 16 people killed in each department. In descending order, the Gard has had 11 fatalities and each of three other departments, eight. The remainder range from seven down to two deaths during the last 15 years and 12 departments suffered a single mortality each during the same period.

The loss of 379 lives sounds a lot and indeed, even a single fatality is one too many, but it must be remembered that, though the overall population of France is similar to that in the UK, there are many more people who participate in sporting shooting over here. Figures suggest that some 1.2 million of the French population is involved in game shooting on a regular basis.

No matter how careful everyone may be, whether their chosen sport is skiing or shooting, it is a sad fact that, accidents, fatal or otherwise are bound to occasionally happen. What does surprise me though, is that so many shooting-related incidents happen in a country where, in order to go out with a gun, anyone who does so will have had to pass the "permis de chasseur". Obtaining a permis involves a quite complicated theoretical and practical test, a part of which covers in considerable detail, potential dangers, an awareness of your immediate surroundings and safe angles at which to shoot.

In the UK, a good deal of game shooting is driven and everyone is taught not to shoot at a pheasant until it is above tree height or sky can be seen around it. Here in France, most of the day-to-day shooting is walked up and the bird shot going away. The angle of flight of such a bird is, therefore, likely to be far less – and potentially more dangerous should anyone be unfortunate enough to be on the other side of the hedge.

Another difference between game shooting in the two countries involves the use of semi-automatic shot-guns. They are permitted in France and even though they are only used by 35 percent of the chasseurs, they seem to be implicated in 43 percent of the shooting-related accidents reported throughout France. If my less than perfect understanding of the French language is correct, that is quite an alarming statistic.

Media articles brought about as a result of the latest findings say that every effort should be made to erect roadside signs and other warnings in order that the public is made aware of the fact that shooting is taking place in a given area. There is also the suggestion made that all, rather than some, chasseurs should wear fluorescent gilets so that they can be more easily seen by fellow sportsmen. At the moment they appear to be favoured mainly by those who shoot large game such as boar rather than anyone such as the commune shooters whose main quarry are pheasants and partridge. One exception is in Doubs, in the Franche-Comté region where all 8,700 chasse members have decided to wear fluorescent "sécurité" jackets for every aspect of shooting – apart from when duck-flighting where camouflage is obviously essential. Even then, in the interests of safety, the federation's rules say that Guns must only stand in a hide or by a fixed peg and not wander around the water's edge at will.

In the UK, I cannot imagine that there is any shooting day which does not begin with a safety talk. In France, from my experience at least, a safety talk given to the various groups of commune shooters before they venture out each day is the exception rather than the norm. It is now being suggested that such talks should be undertaken regularly in order that all Guns should be made aware of all potential dangers associated with sporting shooting.

Tragically, roughly ten percent of all the people who are injured or killed are not actively involved in a day's sport. The fact that much of French land permits almost a "right to roam" scenario does not help. Some of the casualties include woodland mushroom-pickers and even mountain cyclists and one suggestion currently being put forward is that all users of the countryside – and not just members of the chasse – should wear fluorescent jackets when they are out and about during the autumn and winter. Fighting against the need for such precautions are the group known as the "Rassemblement des Opposants à la Chasse" (ROC), an umbrella group which, according to their blurb: "lobbies for the right of the majority of the population to enjoy safe and unthreatened access to the countryside throughout the year, and especially on Sundays".

A fluorescent jacket is rapidly becoming normal attire for the French sportsman – they can be seen, but should the weekend country visitor ensure the same visibility?

A border anomaly
4th April 2007

Something else very different in France is the fact that in some regions it is still possible to shoot roe deer with shotguns, in fact it is permitted in 41 of the 90-odd "départements". Here at "Le Malineau", we border onto both the Maine-et-Loire and Deux-Sèvres, leading to the strange situation whereby, because it's permitted in the Loire and forbidden in Deux-Sèvres, it's theoretically possible to use a shotgun against deer in one half of a wood, but not in the other in places intercepted by regional boundaries!

Much of the argument put forward in favour of retaining the use of shotguns seems to be centred on the safety aspect. The Office Nationale de la Chasse et de la Faune Sauvage (l'ONCFS) have recently released figures showing that the shooting of "grand gibier" (deer, boar etc) with rifles, caused 104 accidents for every million shots fired, whereas the shooting of "petit gibier" (game, hares etc), principally with shotguns, caused "only" 99 injuries for around 30 million shots fired.

A gun-maker demonstrating his skills at a local show.

Apparently, during a four-year period, there were three deaths occurring from 61 accidents involving shotguns compared to 48 fatalities resulting from 267 incidents with rifles. Strange figures to use, but simplified, it seems to work out that five percent of deaths were caused by shotguns, compared to 18 percent where rifles had been involved. All in all, though, I'm not sure that these figures are sufficient reason to continue using shotguns against roe deer but it would take a far better man than me to convince dyed-in-the-wool traditionalists that rifles were the better option!

Ready for the off
21st September 2011

In most of the British Isles it seems traditional for most shoots to meet at nine o'clock and then move off some twenty to thirty minutes later – if that is, you can get your Guns away from chatting and coffee. If you can't and the keeper or person in charge is expecting you on your pegs by 9.30am then there could be trouble – trust me, I know! There are, though, other than the old-established ones about dusk and daylight, as far as I'm aware, no rules or regulations about when exactly the first shot may be fired.

Here in France things are not quite the same and by starting too early, one could fall foul of "article R.424-6 du code de l'environment", which is a piece of government legislation that gives the power to decree a starting time to the department's prefecture. In most departments, this is fixed somewhere between the hours of eight and nine at the start of the season and gets a little later as the year heads towards Christmas. Around "Le Malineau" it is very definitely an eight o'clock start when the season opens sometime near the beginning of September. A little like a military salute, no sooner than the house clock stops striking, is it possible to hear the first shots. In fact they are often so quick off the mark that it seems almost that several of the local chasseurs must have the target in their sights immediately prior to the hour – either that or they all let off a shot purely for the enjoyment of once more being out!

Despite what some might think about the French shooters being happy-go-lucky people ready and willing to take a pot-shot at anything that moves, nothing can be further from the truth and, out of all the European countries, France is arguably the most regulated. Proof of such regulations can usually be found in this month's *Le Chasseur Français* magazine. Predictably, it celebrates the opening of the season and, within its pages, appraises the reader of many pertinent and legal facts. Firstly, one is reminded of the need for the "permis de chasse", after which any information appertaining to the annual national licence to shoot game follows. It has, out of interest, recently gone up roughly seven euros and now costs 209.24€

Should you require a temporary licence, one to cover you for nine days costs 123.26€, whilst if you're only intending a short spell of shooting, it will cost 62.45€ for three. If you stay in your department to shoot, the cost of the temporary licences will set you back either 24.82€ or 16.16€ respectively. Insurance is also important – France loves its rules and regulations – and so, under "article L.423-16", one should have, and be ready to show to a government employed "garde-chasse", a valid certificate. He might also want to check your game book so you need to be filling that in on a regular basis!

Getting the Guns ready for the first drive at the appointed time is not always an easy task!

"Self-policing" works in France
7th February 2007

Not long before the beginning of this current shooting season, the French adopted the new lead-free cartridge legislation that has been in place for some time in the UK. It seems that from snippets which have been appearing in the French press since then, the authorities have been taking the new laws quite seriously and there have been several reports of inspectors checking whether or not shot game has been killed legitimately by non-toxic shot. For a country which makes laws in order to make work and ensure that there is a plentiful supply of paperwork and forms – all of which require completing in duplicate and more often in triplicate, only to then have the rules either bent or ignored by the vast majority of the population, I find this zealousness quite surprising and very much out of character!

With shooting being such a popular sport in virtually all of the rural areas and the fact that there are reckoned to be less than 2,000 "inspectors" directly concerned with implementing the law, it is usually left to the honesty and integrity of the individual. From personal observation, it seems that this "self-policing" works quite well. In fact, for a country where most of the people think that "laws are a good idea, but surely they don't mean me?", the system works staggeringly well and I'm willing to bet that very few sportsmen venture out without, for example, having first obtained the necessary game licence – can the same be said for all game shooters in the UK, I wonder?

"Get off my land!"
26th September 2008

In another life, I write a regular "questions and answers" page for _French Property News_. Given the all-embracing heading of _Rural Riddles_, it is not surprising that my email postbag covers such diverse topics as gardening problems, wildlife identification and the logistics of moving one's guns/ dogs et al to France. One subject that reappears with quite a degree of regularity is the fact that it seems that the local chasse can shoot over any land, no matter whether or not the owner is pro or anti shooting. Understandably, such an assumption is worrying to a number of "ex-pats" who suddenly find their Sunday morning disturbed by the close proximity of gun shot and even, on one occasion, their kitchen full of errant gundogs all intent on stealing their cat's food.

It is generally thought that Guns can shoot on all farmland less than 20 hectares, but on anything over that acreage, they must have the express permission of the landowner. Wildlife reserves and areas on which hunting and/or shooting is officially banned, such as is the case with some parcels of government forestry in France are, of course, out-of-bounds, although in some of the latter mentioned woodland, it is possible for certain people – a hunt, for example, to obtain a special licence to enter. Anyone who wishes to stop shooting enthusiasts from the local commune from entering their land is best advised to start by approaching either the "mairie" or the president of the relevant shooting association before taking it upon themselves to begin erecting "Propriété Privée" or "Chasse Interdite" signs.

Much of the French countryside is shot over – and offers some interesting sport over undulating and spectacular countryside.

At the end of each season, every association holds what might loosely be called an AGM, but is more realistically a meeting of like-minded souls who gather at a suitable village hall or "salle des fêtes" (village hall) in order to partake in a glass or two of wine and have something to eat. They do, however, conduct some serious business and, in the absence of a more direct contact, it is a good place to go to either find out more about shooting in your local area or – to begin negotiations preventing its members on your land in future years.

It is a little disconcerting to read ill-informed articles in some English-speaking papers printed in France, which are obviously the means by which most of us who now live in France gain our knowledge and information. One such appeared recently, the by-line claiming that the author donned "his combat gear to find out what 'la chasse' is all about". Following in the footsteps of a local French friend, they apparently had a good day and a couple of pheasants were shot – which was all well and good until the writer claimed:

"Finally, we retired defeated to a vineyard. The grapes were refreshing. Suddenly three grouse broke cover. Startled, the grouse took off with a "chuk chuk", straight towards us." Grouse in a vineyard – surely not? Do you think he might possibly have meant partridge?

Protection from the antis
16th September 2009

The shooting season is once again in full swing in most parts of France. Whilst there is far less opposition to hunting and shooting here than there is in Britain, there are however, one or two groups that always try to make their presence felt at the beginning of each season.

One such is ASPAS, an organisation that claims to protect the countryside's wildlife and who are petitioning for tighter controls on the French person's traditional field sports, one of which is to ban Sunday shooting. Not that I can see them getting very far with that one as Sunday shooting around the commune is such an integral part of life for most of France's "chasseurs" that there would be a national outcry were it ever to get anywhere near a statute book. The "right of pursuit" is, according to many, an achievement of the Revolution and not one which they are prepared to give up without a fight.

Although they themselves might act responsibly, there is the undoubted possibility that organisations such as ASPAS may spawn further individual protest groups which then go out and attempt to disrupt what is very much a traditional and popular part of French rural life. A recent government law should, however, help protect the sportsperson from such disturbances and now its possible that, if convicted, saboteurs could well face a fine of up to 1,500 euros and may, in certain circumstances, lose their driving licence.

What's in a name?
29th July 2009

Because most organisations in France have such long names and titles, it is more usual for them to be referred to by their initials and as such, are immediately recognised by their acronym. A perfect example is the "Office National de la Chasse et de la Faune Sauvage" (l'ONCFS), an organisation under the supervision of France's ministry of ecology and agriculture. Not only does it have a long name, but it also has plenty of officers and technicians working for it – some 1,639 at the last count! Unlike many government offices however, l'ONCFS does a great deal of good in the French countryside and, although strict in imposing legislation and the like, is nevertheless, very definitely on the side of field sports and the way in which participants manage the habitat.

A subsidiary group is known as the "Surveillience et d'Alertes Sanitaires pour la Faune Sauvage" (SAGIR) and is a national network responsible for the monitoring of wildlife health. It was created in 1986 and a team of veterinary surgeons have been working for the benefit of SAGIR ever since then. Not only do they carry out post-mortems on dead wildlife in an effort to determine the cause, but they also aim to improve their understanding of pathogens (bacteria, viruses, parasites) of wildlife – especially those that may also affect domestic animals. Funded mainly by l'ONCFS and SAGIR Federation "hunter" members, they carry out an average of 3,500 post-mortems and subsequent testing each year. Inevitably, many of their findings on the possible causes of death have been indeterminate, in particular those on deer, hares and pigeon; their research has, nevertheless, solved certain mysteries such as a sudden rise in the deaths of pigeon that began in 1995. After four years of study, it was discovered that the abnormal mortality rate was due to a dressing found only on the seeds of "petits pois" (garden peas). In 2002, they were somewhat quicker off the mark when they discovered that a minor pig "plague" – not swine flu – found in domestic animals had its origins in "sanglier", or wild boar.

Most of the carcasses tested are found mainly by stalkers and game shooters, wardens from l'ONCFS and, in some cases, casual countryside walkers. They contact either their local shooting federation or the nearest ONCFS office and the dead animal or bird is then taken to the nearest veterinary laboratory where it is first given a visual examination in order to find any obvious injuries and parasites. It is then examined internally and various fluid samples are taken and sent to specialist laboratories at Lyon and Reims.

Eventually, all general details (where the animal was found, on what date and the conditions of discovery) and lab results are collected and sent to l'AFSSA (Agence Française de Sécurité Sanitaire des Aliments) where they are used to build up an overall national picture of the state of wildlife welfare. With such attention to detail, no wonder that the last budget made public amounted to 1,239,000 euros!

The National Woodcock Club
22nd November 2006

The chance to shoot a left and right at woodcock is a dream to many British sportsmen, but here in France, there seems to be plenty of opportunity and in some areas shooting woodcock over pointers or spaniels takes precedence over any other kind of sporting shooting. There is even a Club National des Bécassiers, founded in 1951, to study and care for woodcock and their habitat that has its headquarters in Paris and, unlike Great Britain, where to be a member of the Shooting Times Woodcock Club, it is necessary to have shot a left and right, there are no such restrictions on membership.

The CNB use the logo of a bell crossed with the woodcock pin feather. Like those fortunate enough to shoot a woodcock in the UK, French shooters quite often place the pin feather of a shot bird in the band of their hat. Others keep them safe in readiness for the sad day when their favourite woodcock dog departs to the great hunting ground in the sky, at which time the feathers are buried with the animal. Other dog handlers will keep a framed picture containing all the pairs of feathers displayed as trophies recalling each bird pointed and bagged during the lifetime of a good dog.

The relevance of the bell in the logo of the NCB is obviously its connection with the one on the collar of some "chien de bécasse". Although there are countless mass-produced hunting bells on the market, there is still at least one craftsman making woodcock hunting bells by hand. "Les Sonnailles Daban", based in the Pyrenees, claim to be "the only authentic manufacturers of bells from Collioure to Hendaye" and the present owner is the fifth generation descended from Jean-Bernard Daban who set up the original business in 1795.

While still on the subject of the French, woodcock and traditions, the culinary aspect is worth a mention. In some parts of France, Calvados brandy is poured into the bird as soon as it is shot, by means of a small funnel or entonnoir. This supposedly adds to the bird's delicate flavour as it permeates through the flesh in the same way as marinating other game in wine and herbs. Another, far less attractive tradition is this game – to be played at the end of a meal which has woodcock on the menu: "Take an empty bottle of good wine, replace the cork on top and push a pin on top of the cork. Set a cooked woodcock head left over from the meal on the pin and place the bottle at the centre of the table. Ask an innocent hand to push the bill and make the head turn – it is a sort of woodcock roulette. When the head stops, the bill should be pointing at one of the guests. This

"A bird in the hand" or, in this instance, a woodcock in the mouth!

one has the privilege to eat all the heads from the table, but must tell a good story to the others as they light up a cigar and sip their brandy – if you want the story to be good, watch the number of bottles you serve, the right point is the one between generously and too much!"

Ducking the issue
22nd August 2007

I don't know if it is the same throughout the whole of France, but the duck-shooting season begins around here towards the end of August. Most tuck themselves away and flight a pond in much the same way as in Britain but, for generations, some enthusiastic shooters have, quite legally, used a live decoy to attract mallard onto a stretch of water. This year, however, this might not be permitted due to worries regarding avian flu. Protective legislation against the disease not only prevents the transportation of live decoys, but also insists that any wildfowlers who keep ducks expressly for this purpose, must keep their stock in enclosures that do not permit them to have contact with any sort of wild birds.

Daniel and Frederic Guette returning from a duck flight – with their decoy duck in the cat box at the back of the trailer!

The first (and only time) I saw a live decoy in action, I was fascinated. It was when I accompanied father and son Daniel and Frederic Guette to one of their lakes near Chambord, where I was astounded to see them tether a live decoy duck in the shallows by the use of strings and a metal weight anchored into the mud, before then disappearing into a perfectly made hide. At the end of the flight (which was I must admit, not all that successful), the decoy duck was carefully retrieved and placed back in its carrying box – it was apparently, a veteran to the game and spent its summer months in the Guettes' chicken run!

An up-and-coming boar shoot
20th October 2010

A couple of days before my last trip back to England, I went to see Shaun Trenchard. Shaun runs the 100 hectare Parc de Launay not far from Doue la Fontaine in the Loire Valley. Although the place had been a sporting estate for many years and has a huge amount of history attached, it was, until Shaun's intervention, quite neglected and had been used simply as a rich man's playground occupied for just a few weeks in the shooting season. Old woodland rides had been allowed to become overgrown; boar stocks weakened through no selective culling and high seats (such as they were), rotten and unusable.

Under Shaun's stewardship, the old shooting lodge has now been converted into both a comfortable home for him and a wonderfully hospitable place for visiting Guns. It wasn't the best of days when I went to visit, it being wet and breezy, but the shoot room was as warm and welcoming as my host and his new French wife. The next door gun room was a treasure trove of interest: a collection of rifle bullets and shotgun cartridges such as I'd never seen before and on the walls, photos of encounters with boar at, as far as I am concerned, distances far too close for comfort. I know I would never possess the steely nerve required to remain calm on a woodland ride as a huge "sanglier" came steaming towards me.

There are, however, many who do enjoy this adrenalin rush and Shaun's clients return year after year from both France and abroad. I can see why; not only is Shaun most knowledgeable and enthusiastic in his passion for the boar but, as the huge green gates automatically open, you enter a most impressive courtyard, to one side of which is the house and shoot room, to the other a barn which is currently being converted into accommodation for guests. Not just average accommodation either: Shaun tells me that when completed, it will be to the highest standard and include all manner of luxuries right down to the under-heated flooring.

At Parc de Launay, Guns can choose between high-seat and driven boar shooting. The latter sounds fascinating. Hounds are used to separate a boar from a herd which might include a dozen or more members, but it's not as easy as it sounds because when threatened, boar will pack together tightly and some will even lay head to tail around the group forming an almost impenetrable barrier.

Like their distant cousin the domestic pig, wild boar are supremely intelligent and if one that has been hunted before is eventually persuaded to leave the herd, it is not unknown for it to run until it finds another herd and then forcibly push one of those out for hounds to hunt instead. Shaun also tells of having seen a hunted boar take to the icy waters of the lake and, having inhaled air, swim under the ice before crashing through the crust of frozen water and emerging on the other bank where hounds could not follow.

Boar on the estate have bred there for many generations but Shaun now maintains their viability by some selective culling and the occasional introduction of totally unrelated males. Lest you might think it impossible to know every animal on such a place, I have been told that Shaun spends almost every daylight hour watching and/or working on the estate and so very probably does!

Too much of a bad thing
3rd October 2012

As much as I enjoy being involved in all forms of field sports, be it here or in the UK, I must admit to rapidly becoming less enamoured with one particular aspect of the French commune shooting that is carried out around our home at "Le Malineau".

We get the odd pheasant in the hedgerows and plenty of partridge amongst the stubble. As I've mentioned before, normal practice for the Sunday morning Guns is to meet up at a given place and then, after the sometimes quite protracted greetings, they split and wander off in groups of two or three and work their dogs over a given area before meeting back up again at lunchtime. Afterwards, they divide again and each cover ground where they've not been during the morning. As a result, we might have a small team thoroughly working their dogs around the house, field and hedgerows between, say, 9.00-10.00am, followed by another group barely an hour later. Then, after lunch, yet a further group will work the same hedgerows, fields and scrubland during the afternoon (and possibly again in the early evening).

To my mind this is far too much disturbance, especially for the partridges who, by the end of the day, are thoroughly exhausted from being chivvied from place to place – so much so that I've seen them still barely able to fly first thing on Monday when the dog inadvertently disturbs them during our early morning walk.

How things are done in the UK is, in my opinion, far better practice. Rarely are the same birds driven twice in the same day and, if they are, it is only after a considerable rest that enables game birds to regain their body sugar levels and flying strength. As an example, it might be that pheasants are flushed during the first drive of the day (from where they fly to other game crops and coverts) and then, several hours later, maybe as the first drive after lunch, those crops and woods are pushed through towards the standing Guns. Any birds that have been previously driven are thoroughly rested (and will not be disturbed again until the next planned shoot which may be several days or even weeks away); it also means that they are pushed back into the more familiar surroundings of where they were found first thing and where they are probably more used to roosting and feeding.

Where birds are driven to, and how often they are likely to be disturbed during a day's sport should, therefore, be given very careful consideration. So too, should the time when shooting finishes for the day as all game needs to be given plenty of undisturbed time to settle before night falls.

SHOOTING DAYS IN BRITAIN

For over two decades, at the end of each shooting day I diligently completed the estate game book. As one tome became full, the pristine first pages of another were opened and written on in good quality ink and my best hand-writing. Eventually, by the time I'd finished my last day's shooting and was ready to move on to pastures new, there was a library of five impressive-looking volumes; each of which contained information on what woods and game crops had been driven on a particular day, the numbers of pheasant, partridge and "various" shot on each beat, weather conditions, the names of the Guns, the distribution of the bag (how many birds had been sold to the game dealer and how many given away as gifts) and finally, my personal notes and comments.

Although at the time, I felt there might have been better things I could have been doing on the evening of a shoot or at coffee the next morning, looking back over a period of twenty years, those game books proved fascinating reading. From them it was possible to learn that there was, for example, no point in driving a certain wood either immediately after beating through another in the vicinity, or when a specific wind direction prevailed. As I took the hallowed journals from my cottage to the estate office for safe-keeping, I reflected that as well as being of practical use, they might just also prove a record of my time employed there and possibly even offer a little "social history" for future generations. Imagine then, my horror and disappointment when I heard some years later that, after the sale of the estate, "my" game books had been passed on to a new head-keeper who subsequently, and for no obvious reason, decided to make a bonfire of them.

Keeping a tally
1st October 2005
Game books, particularly personal ones, are a wonderful way of reminding oneself of a particular day's sport and, although we all like to recall the "red letter days" when birds flew well and we shot magnificently, it is also quite interesting to recollect the times when things did not go exactly as one would have wished! One particularly grumpy-sounding Gun of yesteryear recorded in his game book for 1935, that a day's shooting had been spoilt by "children and farm stock" but failed to elaborate. In January the following year, the same gentleman bemoaned the fact that an outing planned for 20th January was cancelled because of the "inconsideration" of George V dying on the same date! It is, very definitely, the notes and anecdotes which make a game book special.

Sadly though, it seems from speaking to many Guns, that the collating of a game book is nowadays a minority occupation – which is a great shame when one considers just how much pleasure can be gained from a well-kept personal record. As a friend of mine once quite correctly observed, "… it's not all about ego-massaging, rather the creating of a tangible record of enjoyable days which can then be enjoyed by both the record-keeper and future generations."

The Edwardians considered the killing of large bags to be the essence of a successful shoot – and kept records to prove it. A Sandringham game book of 1905 clearly shows a tally of 1,342 partridges taken on 10 November that year. The 6th Lord Walsingham was known for his love of record bags and would take the keeping of notes appertaining to them very seriously indeed. Not content with a simple game book, his great nephew had it that he tended to register his exploits "… in framed manuscript, with what he took to be suitable illustrations in his own hand – and with evident satisfaction …" How sad Walsingham would have been to learn that his famed and framed grouse record eventually ended its life hanging in the lavatory at Merston Hall. Ralph Payne-Gallwey was also apparently fond of designing and illustrating his own game records for his Thirkleby estate in North Yorkshire – the pages of which contained quite meticulous works of sporting art.

As plain or fancy though a game record might be, I can do no better than record the thoughts E. C. Keith who, in his 1937 book *Gun For Company* had this to say: "… after tea … before a hot fire which makes it almost impossible to keep eyes open and senses alert, the incidents of the day will spring to mind. Then we shall see and recall every shot, every kill and every miss, and inscribe it in that book of memories as a day that was worth while." So, although a legacy from years gone by, the keeping of game books is one tradition that perhaps should be continued by the 21st century Gun, no matter whether they be involved in a grand formal affair or a D.I.Y. rough shoot.

Shooting in the government's forests
8th November 2006

Over a shooting lunch recently, I got talking to a letting agent for the Forestry Commission and it was fascinating to learn just how much has changed from the days when the Commission's primary interests involved timber extraction and any other use of their land was nothing more than a minor "side-line".

It used to be an easy matter to rent for shooting on Forestry Commission ground and, provided that one abided by the conditions laid out on the contract and sent in an annual return form, you were, from my experience at least, left pretty much to your own devices. In the southern region alone, the letting of sporting rights still generates over £½ million each year, but the actual price per hectare ranges depending on what part of the country one lives and also fluctuates in some regions because of demand. Thus it might be possible to find a potential shoot costing only a few pounds per hectare in Scotland whereas in the south-east, the price per hectare is considerably more. Other factors seemingly affect the situation too: for instance, it appears that because Paul McCartney, amongst others, rents Forestry Commission land at a highly inflated price – as much as £70 per hectare – in order to prevent shooting and create a "conservation" area, it is not unknown for land in the same locality to be offered to would-be sporting enthusiasts at a similar rate, which obviously puts it out of the financial range of the average small-scale shooting syndicate.

All the revenue generated from the letting of sporting rights goes to the central offices at Whitehall, but Forestry Commission workers and stalkers, more properly known as "wildlife rangers" in these days of political correctness, are funded regionally from an annual budget. Like many countryside enterprises, there is, therefore, a very valid need for each area to diversify and increase their potential revenue by whatever means possible. Rambling trails, off-road cycling, café franchises all bring in people and much-needed cash, but such activities do, inevitably, curtail the possibility of shooting and stalking tenancies becoming available due to the obvious safety aspect and conflict of interests.

In 2002, the New Forest and the forest of Fontainebleau – the latter covering an area of more than 25,000 hectares and situated south-east of Paris – signed an agreement to share expertise in managing nature conservation, sporting issues and heritage in areas of heavy recreational use. At the time of signing, the Forestry Commission's deputy surveyor for the New Forest said, "Despite the distance between our two forests, we have more in common with each other than we do with other forests in our own countries." Since then, French foresters have visited the New Forest in order to learn the British technique of controlled burning, which is not only necessary on the best-managed grouse moors but is also vital in maintaining large areas of heathland.

A square peg
22nd October 2010

To my mind, there's almost as much anticipation of the day's sport when it comes to actually positioning the gun pegs themselves a week or so before the first day as there is in the day itself. An ex-boss of mine loved going round with me placing pegs. It was a sensible thing to do for it meant that he knew exactly where everything was when it came to the locations intended for his guests to stand, but it was the excitement of preparing for a new season which was his real reason for coming along with me.

Actually when you can position the pegs depends on a multitude of things, not least the progress, or otherwise, of autumn ploughing and whether or not there is livestock in the fields where you wish to place them. If most of the shooting is conducted in woodland then there is no

A white gun peg is far easier to see than the more traditional hazel stick.

problem, but I don't think there can be many shoots that don't have at least one drive over arable land, or where sheep or cattle have access.

Traditionally, shooting pegs should be made of a hazel wand with a number card and there can be nothing more evocative than to see a Gun standing on such a peg with a dog alongside, both waiting in eager anticipation of the first bird. However, far more efficient in terms of being easier to see, less able to be damaged by livestock, and certainly longer-lasting, are the short white painted gun pegs made from lengths of 2"x 2" timber.

Silence is golden
24th October 2007

Anyone experienced in ferreting knows that to approach a set of rabbit holes with a great deal of unnecessary noise is going to alert its occupants and make the subsequent proceedings more difficult than they should be. Likewise, a deer stalker, by the very nature of his title, realizes that crashing about and neglecting to consider the wind direction, for example, is not conducive to getting close to his target. A trout fisherman knows that he is unlikely to catch many fish if he casts his shadow rather than just his fly over the water and does not take advantage of a screen of reeds to shade his form. Why is it then, that the average game Gun, or even, dare I say it, a team of beaters, fails to comprehend the fact that a noisy approach to their peg or whilst lining out in preparation to walking up a field of cover crops is going to have a similar effect?

Contrary to what those of us who have reared and worked with them for several years might, on occasions, think, game birds are not stupid and they still have a great degree of the self-preservation instinct left in their breeding – which is exactly as it should be. They might tolerate a certain degree of disturbance prior to the first day's shooting, but once they are aware that any undue noise spells danger, they are off to find a safer environment. Many is the time in the past that I have taken a brace of birds to a neighbour whose garden encroaches onto the estate on the day after we had been out only to be told "oh yes, even if you'd not given us a list, we would have known you were shooting yesterday because our garden was full of birds." We might not have been anywhere near that particular part of the shoot the previous day, but the pheasants had obviously heard the disturbance and drifted out of harm's way. It is, it must be admitted, easier to get away with things in the early part of the season, but by Christmas many gamekeepers find that, despite having employed many beaters, they are actually short in the line due to the fact that they have found it necessary to deploy several of them as "stops".

There are not many shoots that employ a totally separate team of "stops" nowadays; nevertheless, in my time, I have been involved with shoots where the "stops" team met at daybreak and were delegated their duties. They would be taken to a point where game was known to leak from the corner of a wood or down a hedgerow leading from a cover crop and left there for several hours before it was time to drive their particular beat. Quite often, the drive was not due to take place until late morning or, as on one shoot in North Yorkshire where the head-keeper used to put his wife out as a "stop", even the first drive after lunch – but perhaps there was a hidden agenda there! "Stops" of some description are, however, still a very important aspect of a successful driven day: they will prevent birds wandering, either due to their natural foraging routine or as a result of being disturbed by beaters on a nearby drive or, most likely, the sound of guns.

The Guns themselves, especially those for whom a day out is merely a social occasion, and therefore sometimes have little or no understanding of the difficulties involved in running a shoot, can often be their own worst enemy – it is difficult enough driving birds over the line without the extra trials and tribulations brought about by a team of noisy Guns. How can they expect a plentiful supply of good high-flying game over the line when, in order to reach their peg, they have slammed vehicle doors; lost their dog and shouted and whistled for its return, as well as having had a conversation with the Gun next door but one – some 100 yards away? Pheasants and partridges living in the next county will have been alerted to their presence … let alone those in the next drive.

To my mind, one of the best ways of preventing too much noise is to limit the amount of vehicles used on the shoot. The beaters are not a problem as, traditionally, they have always been transported from drive to drive in a communal trailer. It is, however, becoming increasingly common for the pickers-up team to use their own vehicles. Their wish to do so is quite understandable: there is no danger of the dogs getting into a fight as might be the case if they were all confined in the back of a single vehicle and, for the owners, it is far preferable that they have immediate access to their wet weather clothing and any other paraphernalia deemed necessary throughout the course of the day. Separate vehicles also means that the team captain can delegate certain pickers-up to stay behind in order to thoroughly sweep through whilst other team members push on in preparation for the next drive. Make sure, however, that they are given strict instructions as to where and when they can park – it would not be the first time that a row of pickers-up vehicles have turned birds back over the heads of beaters blanking in a piece of ground.

Guns are definitely a breed apart – and I know that any professional keepers reading this will identify with what I say. Allow them to use their own vehicles and some will be left behind, despite having all driven off in convoy together; get lost despite having assured the host that they know exactly which is the next drive and, on arrival at the drive, will suddenly realize that they left their gun in the back of another person's car who has since been delegated the position of "back gun". A Gun's trailer, provided that it conforms to safety standards and is fitted out with racks for weapons

Guns who use their own vehicles are far more likely to disturb game than are those who travel together in the shoot trailer – and low voices are the essence when it comes to explaining the details of a particular drive.

and a shelf for cartridges and wet weather gear, keeps everyone together –
and cuts down on noise.

Going deaf
4th February 2009

By coincidence, and for totally unconnected reasons, the conversation on
recent shooting days has included much discussion on deafness. Some,
it must be said, has been more forceful than others, as on a recent day
in Wiltshire when by the time the keeper had finished one of his rants,
no-one – no matter how deaf they claimed to be – could have failed to
hear his instructions nor what he thought of us; including the fact that it
appears that very few of us had married parents at the time we were born!

Deafness is, however, a very serious problem amongst many shooting
folk and it is not all down to the fact that we are getting older. Apparently,
if you were to take the roar of a motorcycle running full-throttle for
40 hours non-stop and then condense it into a split second, you have,
according to the experts, a very good approximation of the sound energy
generated by an average gunshot. So, unless you have been sensible and
used ear defenders throughout your shooting life, every single shot taken
means that, as the years have progressed, we have all been getting slightly,
but permanently more deaf.

Now in my mid-fifties, I think that it's true to say that hardly anyone of
my generation ever wore hearing protection of any kind and if you did, you
were looked on as being slightly odd and precious. Never as interested in
shooting as I was the other aspects of gamekeeping and the shooting day,
I put the fact that the deafness in my left ear was due to the fact that I'd
stood for many hours loading double guns for my various employees and
their friends, but at a dinner in Sussex recently, a fellow guest (a doctor)
told me that shooting from the right shoulder would most likely result in
the left, rather than the right ear being affected – quite literally a case of
"going in one ear and out of the other".

Scientists have proven that it takes very little "sonic trauma" to cause
permanent damage and that for every five years of recreational shooting
a person enjoys, the risk of high-frequency hearing loss escalates by some
seven percent. The reasons given are, apparently, all to do with the cochlea –
a fluid-filled, snail shell–shaped organ buried deep in the inner ear. Sound

A set of ear-defenders should be part of every Gun and loaders' shooting equipment. (Photo: Elliot Hobson)

travels through the air as pressure waves that are then directed down the ear canal to the eardrum, which vibrates. Its slight movements are relayed via three miniature bones (the hammer, stirrup and anvil) to another membrane that covers the opening of the cochlea. When this membrane begins to dance, the vibrations are transmitted inside the cochlea's fluid-filled centre which is lined with minuscule hair-like projections called cilia that are adversely affected by high-frequency sounds. Intense noise, such as a shotgun blast, can cause vibrations so violent that they can, in effect, fell the affected cilia like an earthquake does trees.

Although impossible to totally eliminate the sound of gunshot, you can reduce it to a safer level – apparently and according to researchers, approximately 80 decibels – by the use of well designed ear defenders, or even custom-fitted earplugs. Like many others, it is perhaps too late for me to take effective preventative measures, but if you are responsible for the well-being of newcomers to shooting, never let them stand anywhere near a gun without first of all being equipped with adequate protection.

February pigeon
26th January 2011

When I was a keeper's lad in North Yorkshire, it was a tradition for all the shoots in the area to man the woods on the first Saturday in February in order to keep the pigeon on the move. By doing so, some excellent shooting could be had as the birds moved from wood to wood in an attempt to roost for the night.

Whilst I know that some areas of the country still carry out this practice, it seems to be a little less common than it once was, which is a great shame as, not only is it a legacy from by-gone days, but it is an exciting and evocative sport. Although it is now exactly 40 years since I first had the opportunity to go roost shooting at the end of the game season, I can remember the event as if it was only last week.

On the head keeper's instructions, I'd been out the week before and trimmed out two rough "hides" in some holly bushes, one of which was to accommodate a friend of our employer; the other the head keeper and myself. On the Saturday afternoon the three of us walked across the fields in a flurry of snow accompanied by the keeper's dog Dinah and two extremely hyperactive Springer's belonging to the guest Gun.

Tucked away and ensconced in our makeshift hides, the shooters in the other woods were doing a good job of ensuring that the pigeons kept on the move and it was only a matter of minutes before we started making inroads into our cartridge stocks. The snow kept falling and the birds kept coming, until, an hour or so later, we were shooting in a white-out. Fortunately, the firs kept much of the under-story clear of snow and the dogs were busy picking up the fallen.

Eventually dusk fell and we decided to leave in order to allow the pigeon a chance to come into roost undisturbed. Having picked up and placed the shot birds into a hessian sack – which was, of course, my job to carry – we walked out from the cover of the wood and into fields that had become so covered in snow that we were, for a time, well and truly disorientated. Striking for home, we followed in one another's footsteps much like King Wenceslas's page-boy whilst the dogs could only move by plunging through the snow in much the manner of rabbits hopping through a muddy quagmire!

Hanging game
26th September 2007

One thing I do not understand about the French is their general reluctance to hang game or indeed any type of meat for any length of time. Last Sunday evening we were invited to the home of the infamous Maurice in order to partake of what he had shot that day – so fresh was it that I doubt whether the heart had stopped pumping before the bird was eviscerated! Despite their love of natural food, it appears that the majority of French rural dwellers do not believe in hanging game – perhaps it's a result of living in a warmer climate, but, nevertheless, any game shot over here tends to be eaten within hours, rather than days, of being killed. Personally, I, like Nimrod [a fellow countryside writer], think that "un-hung game is as tasteless and bland as ... chickens found on the supermarket shelves" and is "... only game when it has been hung for a period ..."

Hanging game for a few days will undoubtedly increase the flavour and tenderise the meat. Just how long you hang it depends on how "gamey" you like your meat to taste; what type of game you're hanging (a grouse, for instance, will taste much stronger after being hung for three days than will a pheasant or partridge given the same amount of time) and the weather conditions (thundery weather can turn a bird rapidly, even if the temperature is not high). In warm weather, two or three days might be all that is required, but, during an exceptionally cold period, a week or even up to ten days would not be too long. Find a cool place to hang your game and, in the early part of the season – as we are now – try draping them with muslin and securing with rubber bands in order to protect against flies.

At the risk of teaching "grandmother to suck eggs", traditionally, game birds are hung by their heads whilst rabbits, hares and the carcasses of boar or venison are hung by their back legs, heads facing downwards. Hares are unusual in that they are normally hung with their guts still in, whereas rabbits, boar and deer have their intestines removed as soon as possible after being killed.

Wild duck are not generally hung as, for some reason, the practice does not seem to improve their flavour, but if you have a particular yearning to do so, they, unlike pheasants and partridge, are normally hung by their feet.

As an exception to the rule, whether they be in the UK or France, pigeons are generally plucked, dressed "fresh" and do not require hanging.

Most types of game benefits from being hung for a short while – even if it's only when on sale outside the local butcher's shop.

A place from which to shoot
24th April 2013

When I used to work on the grouse moors, one of the spring-time jobs undertaken about this time of year was the renovating or re-building of the butts in which the Guns would stand come August. Thinking of that quite satisfying occupation recently caused me to wonder about where the word "butt" comes from as, in field sports, we use it not only in connection with the grouse moors, but also sometimes when talking of hides around a flight pond.

There are several English place-names that include the word "Butt" – such as in Barker Butts near Coventry, or Newington Butts in South London and it is from their origins that one might begin to discover how grouse butts eventually came to be given this title.

Seemingly it is all to do with the archery skills required by soldiers in the Middle Ages. In 1252, a law was passed that required all men aged between 15 and 60 to equip themselves with a longbow and arrows. In 1363, a second law made it compulsory that all such men should practice with bow and arrow every Sunday. With no organisation, these training sessions apparently resulted in a great many injuries as a result of arrows being haphazardly "loosed" and so it was eventually decided that special training areas should be designated on the outskirts of towns and villages. These places were called the "Butts", on which were built several circular, turf-covered, flat-topped mounds. On the top of each mound, which was between two to eight metres across and one to three metres in height, was placed the target.

Although obviously ancient in its origin, the word "butt" in connection with the grouse moors and similar was not used extensively until the 20th century. Whilst it was mentioned by A. Stuart Wortley in 1894 in connection with grouse shooting in North Yorkshire, and was an accepted term in Scotland in 1897, throughout his chapter on grouse shooting in the Badminton Library of 1889, Lord Walsingham constantly refers to what we now know as a butt as a "battery" and a line of butts as being a "range of batteries". A few years later, Sir Ralph Payne-Gallwey, author of *Letters to Young Shooters* (published in 1892), talked of "shelters, sometimes rather absurdly called boxes or batteries".

Thinking about it logically, there was, before that time, no need for any such term as it was only around then that driven grouse shooting became popular and places in which Guns could stand were required. In his book *The Wandering Gun* (1960) J. K. Stanford wrote of the fact that many sportsmen of the late 1800s thought "this new fangled grouse driving is fraught with danger" and went on to describe a row of circular grouse-butts "of which a portion of the rim on the right-hand side is raised two feet higher than that on the left, built up with a shot-proof layer of peat-sods. This device effectively prevented the occupant from swinging his gun laterally to his right, and if he were criminal enough to point his gun towards the butt on his left the occupant of that particular pew had two solid feet of parapet to shield him."

4

Gamekeepers and Gamekeeping

THE gamekeeper in France is very different to the tweed-suited person encountered in Britain – at least as far as the government-employed gamekeeper is concerned. Such a "garde chasse" here is typically, a uniformed official and seems to be looked upon with the same contempt as a UK traffic warden. So it is that whenever I've tried to explain my previous job in England, French sportsmen cringe in the same way as I do when seeing a rat! I am now becoming used to it, but in the local bar one evening, I met a new neighbour who responded to my previous profession with particular venom.

All was going well, we chatted about life and the fact that we both had chickens and a tidy vegetable garden. We discussed the fact that we both owned spaniels – in his case, Brittany's, in mine, cockers. We then realized that both of us enjoyed shooting and yet it was from thereon in that things began to go wrong.

I would have thought it a "good thing" to mention that I used to be a gamekeeper in a past life; but no, my new neighbour, a "commune" shooter and deer rifle expert, thought otherwise. In his mind, and obviously, in that of many others, a gamekeeper of the type known in France was, very definitely, a "bad thing". There are of course, keepers employed on some of the big shoots: several of whom are, in fact, British, but the majority are, as I say, government employees and, as such, have a great deal of authority.

Changing times ... or not?
2nd May 2007

How some things do change! In the late 1960s and early 1970s when I first became interested and involved in gamekeeping, shooting rights in south-east England could be had for 25p per acre; each pheasant or partridge shot would have cost you £4.00 to produce and the services of a full-time gamekeeper could be had for around £1,800 per annum. Gamekeeper's jobs were still relatively easy to find and, from Christmas until February, it was possible to look through several pages of adverts in the "Situations Vacant" column of any sporting magazine and almost literally pick and choose the type of position required in the area most desired.

Today, the chance of falling easily into a gamekeeper's job is minimal and for those lucky enough to be employed full-time in such a way, there are things to consider that were unknown of thirty-plus years ago. In an increasingly litigious society, it is nowadays necessary to worry about completing risk assessments and to spell out the obvious to those participating in a day's shooting in order to avoid the possibility of being sued as a result of a beater tripping over barbed wire or cutting his thumb on the edge of a particularly sharp leaf of maize (whatever happened to self-care and commonsense?).

In the early 1970s, I'd venture to suggest that the anti-blood sports' groups were not so vehement. The British Field Sports Society (BFSS) had, however, recently created their "Fighting Fund", but that was only ever intended to be used to fight a possible ban on hunting as, never in anyone's wildest dreams, could it ever be considered that shooting might come under threat. The British Association for Shooting and Conservation (BASC) was still known by everyone as "WAGBI" (The Wildfowler's Association of Great Britain and Ireland) and was primarily involved in what its title suggested. The Game and Conservation Wildlife Trust were known simply as the Game Conservancy and concerned itself solely with research into game rearing, the control of disease and the general well being of the driven game shooter. There was no Countryside Alliance or National Gamekeeper's Organisation (NGO) and certainly no "NOBs" (National Organisation of Beaters and Pickers-up).

The fact that these organisations have changed names, become affiliated, amalgamated, created, or felt the need to add the word "Trust" to their letter-headings in order to emphasize the scientific and conservation aspect of their work, is definitely a sign of how some things have changed in the thirty-odd years since I went to my first job in 1971. Every single one is a worthwhile cause and our support can only help to ensure the future of shooting either financially or by encouraging newcomers to the sport. There are, though, those who feel that the increase in organizations over the past ten years or so is not necessarily a good idea and that the choice dilutes support and finance. Detractors would wish for just one umbrella group that looks after the needs of each individual, no matter what their chosen field sport, but the administration of such a group would surely be a nightmare? To my mind, it is better that we nowadays have more organizations looking after our interests than just the two or three of 30 years ago.

Thankfully, some other changes are also beneficial: the big professionally run shoots still exist, but are being joined by many more small amateur shoots who, by renting some un-wanted parcels of estate land on the outskirts of the bigger shoots, the Forestry Commission, or from interested farmers, manage to keep the sport of shooting very much alive. The latter are run mainly on a D.I.Y. basis by a group of enthusiastic and like-minded friends, who quite often carry out the keepering duties on a rota system. In other cases, members might employ a part-time gamekeeper throughout the year or full-time between the busy months of July and January. Some are in the shoot because, even though they could easily afford to take a full Gun elsewhere, they have no wish to shoot large bags and get a much greater pleasure from being involved on a daily basis.

No matter how they are formulated, every one of these shoots and those involved in their smooth running has always made a significant contribution to the countryside's flora and fauna in all manner of incidental ways. Woodland management, coppicing and the creation of shooting rides benefit no end of birds, insects and butterflies; game crops provide winter cover and seeds to birds and hares; flight ponds are a haven for all manner of waterfowl and the regular feeding of game birds via hoppers or hand has proved a literal life-saver to thousands of song birds weakened by a particularly severe winter.

Shooting and hunting have shaped the British countryside as we see it today and we are benefiting from the foresight of our predecessors. It

Game shooting offers sport, camaraderie and a chance to chat.

is important that we continue to plant woodland, hedges and ensure that safe nesting sites remain.

Perhaps, apart from spiraling costs and the scaling down of gamekeeper numbers, things haven't changed that much in 30 years after all? It's possibly more a case of "the more things change, the more they stay the same", or, as my French neighbours might say, "Plus ça change, plus c'est la meme chose".

It could only be America!
27th October 2007

Whilst bizarre enough to be considered an April Fools' joke at the appropriate time of year, the following is actually true. Earlier this year, two American shooting enthusiasts, Ken Foster and Ralph Brendle, hit upon the crack-pot idea of creating a method and apparatus for waterproofing game birds! Not only that, they were so convinced that their brainchild was such a good one that they decided to apply for a patent to protect their invention. United States patent application number 11/252364 describes, in the most incredible convoluted jargon, exactly what Foster and Brendle submitted to the relevant authorities:

"A system for waterproofing live game birds, the method comprising: providing an apparatus having a spray system and a holding device, said spray system having at least one container for housing a waterproofing composition and at least one spray nozzle secured to at least one container to disperse the waterproofing composition from a position above the holding device and at least one second spray nozzle positioned to disperse the waterproofing composition from a position below the holding device; heating the waterproofing composition in the at least one container to a desired temperature range; loading the game birds into the holding device; placing the holding device in the apparatus; and spraying the birds with the waterproofing composition in a manner that the birds are coated with sufficient waterproofing composition to waterproof them while still permitting the game birds to fly."

As I read through Foster and Brendle's application with growing disbelief, I couldn't help but wonder what the panel of BBCTV's Dragon's Den programme would have made of the idea had they have tried submitting it to them!

Patrice "shuts up shop"
10th August 2011

Patrice, the owner of our local game farm, has decided that this current rearing season will be his last. Despite there being more and more birds being reared and released in France over the past decade or so, things are not always easy for the small-scale breeder and Patrice is not alone in finding it difficult to make a living and is, as a result, "shutting up shop" or, to use a French expression "pushing his keys under the door". Patrice cites a variety of reasons why, in the four-year period between 2006 and 2010, his particular game rearing enterprise has suffered. These range from the fears of Avian flu, the rising cost of feed and production, the economic climate as regards sterling versus the euro (Patrice regularly sold day-old chicks and eggs to the UK) and the harshness of the last two winters which affected us here in our part of France almost as much as it did in Britain.

Generally though, the French game rearing business seems quite healthy as far as the larger producers are concerned. There are reckoned to be at least 14 million pheasants, five million partridges (both grey and red-leg) and a million mallard reared and released annually onto both private and commercial shoots, as well as via the many shooting groups to be found in almost every commune; all of which have to be supplied by someone. In addition, there are birds and eggs exported to other countries – Eric Poullain, president of the "Syndicat national des producteurs de gibier de chasse" (which is, I suppose, France's nearest equivalent to the Game Farmers' Association), reckons that "the breeding of game … generates 200 million euros, 50 million of which is directly a result of exports."

France is thought to have around 12,000 people involved with commercial game rearing in one way or another. There are, however, only 5,000 professional game farmers and, surprisingly, only around 400 are members of the SNPGC. Other figures are equally interesting: take for instance, the fact that 104,000 tonnes of game food is consumed by reared birds each year; 500,000 pheasant hens produce 35 million eggs and that 400,000 pairs of partridge lay 25 million eggs annually. As far as the rearing of mallard is concerned, of those produced, 20 percent of the total is sent to Belgium, England, Spain and Portugal, whilst the remainder is released onto French estates and waterways between May and July.

Many gamebird chicks from France end up being reared on British sporting estates.

The increase in the exporting of game abroad in the form of eggs or day-old chicks has been a gradual thing. Denis Bourasseau, owner of one of the largest game farms says that, "I made my first contact in England in 1991 when I supplied a shoot there with red-leg partridges. The next year they wanted pheasants … which was a lovely surprise. Some months after my first exportation of pheasants, the clients told me that my birds were superb and my business has slowly increased in the UK mainly by word of mouth." Somewhat bizarrely considering the fact that many UK shoots have seen fit to buy their birds from France in an effort to improve existing stocks in Britain, the French much admire traditional British pheasants and aim to produce similar birds which are, as M. Bourasseau describes them "just the right side of wild".

Economics or ethics?
6th February 2013

Until a couple of years ago, Patrice, my friend and occasional bar/tabac drinking partner owned a game farm just a few kilometres away from "Le Malineau" but gave it up due to economies of scale and the fact that the ever-increasing feed and heating costs made him unable to compete price-wise with some of the far larger game farms elsewhere in the Loire and the Vendee – all of whom seem to be doing well because of their ability to negotiate discounts due to bulk ordering.

Figures vary but it seems to be generally accepted that half of the pheasants and 90% of the red-leg partridges reared and released in Britain are imported (mainly as eggs and, to a lesser degree, day-olds). Further estimates have it that 70% of these pheasants and 100% of partridges originate from intensive systems in France and other parts of Europe.

In some cases, certain elements of these laying and rearing systems would not be allowed in Britain and are most certainly frowned upon by most UK game rearers. However, the fact remains that such rearing methods are more acceptable in France and therefore means that greater numbers can be produced at a cheaper cost – and the cheaper costs mean that, even when taking into account the expense of transport, game birds that originate from here can often be bought less expensively by British shoots than can those which are reared on home turf. For example, a couple of seasons ago, it was reported that day-olds from France cost as little as

40p, while those hatched in the UK had a price tag of anywhere between 80p and £1.00. No wonder then that game rearers and estates with books to balance continue to take the economical option wherever possible.

Most French game farms or importers of French stock would prefer to sell eggs rather than chicks or poults because of the EU travel restraints on transport of livestock. As far as freshly-hatched chicks are concerned, they seemingly have a travel time limit of 24 hours (provided the journey is completed within 72 hours of hatching), whereas the permissible journey time allowed for poults is half this; thus placing many parts of Britain out of reach for some of the central and southerly situated French game farmers.

The importation of game bird stocks from France into the UK, although eminently sensible on paper does, it must be admitted, cause ethical worries about the system in which most breeding stock is kept – and newly hatched birds reared. Back in 2008, the Farm Animal Welfare Council (FAWC) produced a report entitled *Opinion on the Welfare of Farmed Gamebirds*, a part of which expressed concern about such techniques. In 2009, the Game Farmer's Association (GFA) was quoted as saying that, "The methods of importing gamebirds needed to be revised." Only last year, a study centred on French gamebird farms suggested that their crowded and intensive conditions might contribute to the spread of bird flu (although the study mainly concerned itself with "wild" duck reared on these establishments, scientists sampling mallard there apparently discovered a high infection rate of a certain strain of bird flu that was not present in truly wild ducks).

As to whether importing European gamebirds into the UK is a good thing or a bad one, there are definitely conflicts of opinion. Looking at the websites of several British game farmers, it seems that some are increasingly trying to source red-leg eggs locally but openly admit to having to occasionally import them in order to meet demand and bring in new blood. Others, however, say that they do not see any need at all to look abroad for stock and promise that their birds are produced by traditional, not intensive methods.

A fine philosophy
10th June 2009

There's an expression used by Romany gypsies to describe their way of life. They call it "living lightly on the land" and employ it to explain the fact that they stay a short while in a place, take a little of what the countryside has to offer them and then move on before denuding an area of its resources. It is a fine philosophy and one which I thought might be as equally suited to certain aspects of game rearing.

It will not be many weeks now before the first poults are being taken to wood. Obviously this necessitates the use of release pens, the interior of which should contain a mixed selection of trees and shrubs, sheltered areas and grassy sunning spots. They should also be large enough to contain the numbers of pheasants intended to be released there, but I'm sorry to say that, from my experience, they seldom are. To be fair, a pen adequate to happily contain 1,000 birds or more is a huge undertaking and very expensive to build if it were constructed to idyllic measurements. In normal years, although not recommended, it is usually possible to get away with a little bit of over-stocking but should the summer prove wet, the pen will very quickly become muddy and an ideal environment for disease.

It is amazing how quickly pheasant poults can strip a pen of vegetation – one minute you're looking at it thinking that your newly released birds will get lost in there and the next you can, by getting down on hands and knees, see from one end to the other. In most instances, the undergrowth will recover, but not if you use the same pen year in year out; in which case, the land will never recuperate, and you will most certainly not be adhering to the gypsy philosophy.

At one time, release pens were not the well constructed edifices they are now and were often nothing more than a few rolls of six foot wire netting run around a clump of trees, pegged at the bottom and protected from foxes by the addition of an electric wire. They were quite often used as a means of holding small quantities of birds reared under broody hens and so didn't need to be very big. They were also almost always taken down and moved from year to year. Such a system was used at my first employment as an under-keeper and it was my job to erect, dismantle and re-erect elsewhere in the same wood during the following spring – by which time there was little or no evidence of a pen ever having been there the previous summer. It is a method well worth still considering today, especially on the smaller D.I.Y. shoot.

Likewise, temporary sectional pens intended for the release of partridges or ducks onto a flight pond should always be built big enough to comfortably house their occupants. Environment-wise, it is not so important because partridges, for example, will most likely be released from pens on stubble or in the corners of game crops which will be ploughed at a later date, but in an effort to prevent disease, it is crucial.

"Living lightly on the land" is not a bad adage to bear in mind – no matter with what aspect of shooting, or indeed, any field sport, you happen to be involved.

Something for nothing
7th June 2007

The estate offers much for nothing when it comes to providing a natural bounty of benefit to the gamekeeper. It is the wrong time of year to select and cut a few stems from the hedgerow for decent walking sticks but in the early autumn, although they are "green", some beating sticks can be cut from a convenient hazel coppice for the shoot helpers who forget to bring their own. They also make decent shanks for flags and a whole army of very

Coppicing a "stand" of chestnut for making release pen posts costs nothing – and creates new and very beneficial growth.

effective partridge flags can be made for nothing by cutting plastic feed bags to size and nailing them to hazel sticks with broad-headed felt nails.

Hazel is useful in other ways too. Long, straight "wands" are ideal as gun pegs and, if the tops are carefully slit down the centre with a knife, hold a peg number perfectly. To prevent the numbers from blowing out in a gust of wind, bind both the top and bottom part of the slit with thin wire or insulating tape. Incidentally, if your food manufacturer cannot or will not, provide you with a few sets of plastic numbers and the shoot treasurer is too tight to permit their purchase from a shooting suppliers, playing cards make a perfect substitute and will last at least one full season. In addition, the fortunate fact that hazel tends to grow relatively straight and has some forks in its growth, makes it perfect for use as sewelling pegs.

Hedgerows not only provide sticks for the shooter and beater, but also the basic ingredients for his or her hip flask! Sloes, damsons, blackberries and elderberries are obvious candidates although it will be necessary to wait a couple of months yet before they begin to appear.

In early June though, there are some less obvious harvests to be had. If you're rearing a few game birds in the back garden as part of your agreement with the shoot, the addition of a few greenstuffs thrown into the pen will not come amiss and will certainly benefit the diet of young pheasants or partridges; as well as helping to prevent feather pecking – often the result of boredom. If you are a keen vegetable gardener, then you'll probably have enough greenstuffs in the form of lettuce gone to seed, or the outer leaves of crops trimmed before they go into the kitchen. If not, it is surprising what the verges of an infrequently used country lane can produce in the shape of vegetation that will be eagerly consumed by part grown game birds. Provided that they are free of agricultural or car-exhaust chemicals, offer your birds dandelion leaves, plantains, shepherd's purse, watercress and, appropriately enough, chickweed and they will definitely benefit from nature's natural bounty.

Keeping birds amused
27th July 2011

Many years ago I was persuaded into buying seed-blocks to which minerals and an attractive aniseed smell had been added. Their manufacturer claimed that they would prevent birds from wandering but in practice, I found that these blocks tended to attract roe deer rather more than they did any wandering pheasants!

Normally a regular feeding routine will help keep birds hanging around. However, in late July and August (and indeed, into September), there is a great deal of natural food to be had – all of which seems to be more attractive to the rapidly-growing pheasants than anything they might find in a strategically-placed hopper or thrown out of the keeper's feed bag as he walks or drives down his feed rides.

In such situations, it may pay to think laterally and rather than using food as an enticement, consider other ways to keep birds amused and from wandering. Easily accessible watering points are one way: especially when the weather is dry and the only water available is that which has been put out for their benefit. It might be time-consuming for the D.I.Y. shoot which, because of finances, will only be able to use homemade drinkers that obviously need regular filling – and totally impracticable for the larger shoot where water is supplied automatically to a line of drinkers sited through the release pen.

Straw bales are a tried and tested traditional way of keeping pheasants amused and one only has to look over a freshly harvested and baled stubble field in the early morning to see birds standing atop the bales of straw. Unfortunately, unless you are able to ask the farmer specifically to provide them, it is nowadays virtually impossible to buy small bales as most farmers use the big round type, or the even larger square ones. If you can get hold of the small ones and are able to place them alongside a sheltered sunny spot somewhere near where you wish the birds to stay, they will prove very useful in keeping pheasants amused.

More so if, instead of providing a line of bales several yards apart and only one bale high, you place one bale on top of another, this lay-out seems very popular with game which will happily use it as a vantage point. In the hope of keeping their birds amused, old keepers used to spend a great deal of time creating attractive-looking stacks of straw in which they would mix tail-endings from the grain store floor. I've tried similar experiments over the years and all that seems to happen is that the straw gets damp, the tailings end up germinating and that vermin such as squirrels and rats are encouraged. In an effort to prevent your neighbours reaping the benefits of all your hard releasing work, though, almost anything is worth trying!

Straw on the feed rides can help keep young poults amused.

A time and a place
17th July 2013

Mid-July, and the time when most people will have this year's poults in the release pens – or will they? There seems to be a trend on some shoots to release birds a little later than is traditional, at least according to a number of keepers and shoot managers. There are a variety of reasons given. For instance, one keeper deliberately ordered late birds from the game farm because of the bad weather throughout winter and spring – a factor that resulted in the farmer planting his crops later than usual. Planted late, it's reasonable to assume that harvest will be late, and this particular keeper was worried about his poults wandering before the cereal crops could be gathered in. Someone else maintains that, as a result of wing-tagging, he's discovered that he gets a better return on birds released slightly later in the summer than is generally accepted, whilst another says that, because of the decreasing daylight hours in the early autumn, late-released birds have less time to wander.

There are two questions to ask, the first of which is, are the "late" birds six or seven weeks of age when released, or are they slightly older and therefore more mature? The second question (and it's not unrelated to the first) must be to do with what time of the season a particular estate is intending to have its first day's shooting.

When I first began keepering in the early 1970s, the majority of shoots didn't begin their season's sport until early to mid-November or, as was often quoted, "when most of the leaf is off the trees". However, more and more shoots are nowadays beginning their season earlier – quite often for legitimate commercial reasons and the need to get in as many days as are practicable. Guns can be selective and leave an immature bird which flies over them but generally, everyone wants to see strong fliers and well-feathered birds on the first day. The time of summer when these pheasants are released (and the age they are when released) will obviously have some bearing on this. Arguably, I think that, in an ideal world, birds should be around 21 weeks of age by the time of the first shoot.

Very large estates, of which there are not so many nowadays, are lucky in that they can stagger their release times, and the parts of the estate on which pheasants were released early can be shot over first whilst areas where birds didn't go to the pens until August (or even September) are left quiet until December. This is not, however, an option for most shoots, although some might be fortunate enough to be able to concentrate on game covers at the beginning of the season and only venture to wooded areas towards Christmas. Even so, the birds encouraged to the game crops obviously need to be adult in looks and strength.

Some keepers say that feeding late-released birds pellets for longer will help them mature and feather more quickly. A high-protein specifically manufactured diet is most certainly beneficial in the development of bone, muscle and feather but will undoubtedly affect the annual shoot budget. There's also the added problem of the likelihood of wet weather as autumn approaches and if one hand feeds rather than uses hoppers, pellets will quickly disintegrate if left on the ride for any length of time.

The mention earlier of wing-tagging proving that, for one keeper, late-released birds tend to wander over less distance is an interesting one. Wing-tagging is an excellent way of learning about the habits of pheasants in general and what happens to them on your ground in particular. There has even been at least one bizarre situation where more un-tagged than tagged birds were shot over a season. Presumably, although the tagged birds must have wandered, they were replaced by un-tagged ones from neighbouring estates; either that or there were an extraordinary amount of wild birds hatched that year!

Tags vary and range from traditional metal ones, to ones which look similar in design to the tags fitted to new clothes. Differently coloured tags will help in enabling you to record many factors: for example, if poults from one particular pen do better than others, how far they wander, whether a new strain introduced to the shoot does better than an old one and, provided that the tags are printed with a year date, how old birds are when you shoot them (or catch them up) in subsequent seasons. One instance recounted to me recently mentioned that, on one shoot, a hen bird was six years old when she was shot – and on the ground some two miles away from where she was released. It reminded me of a time many years ago when I had a spell of wing-tagging all my birds and was one day picking-up on a shoot about six miles away from home.

I'd got into the habit of automatically running my fingers down the edge of each wing as I transferred birds shot on my days to the game larder and so, without thinking, did the same on this occasion to a pheasant one of my spaniels had just retrieved. My mind registered a green tag and the fact that the bird had come from "Adam's Hill" pen. It was not until a minute or so later that I realised that I wasn't on my shoot and that

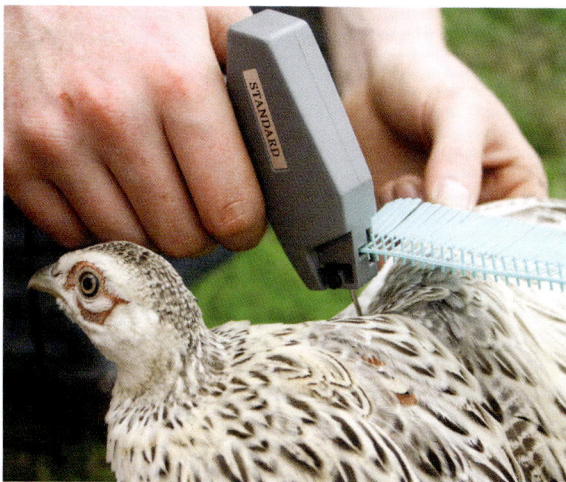

*Wing-tagging can have educational benefits – and also cause some sleepless nights!
(Photo: Mike Swan)*

85

this pheasant was a very long way from home. It also had to have passed through two other shooting estates before it reached the one on which I was picking-up. As one keeper said when I told him this story at the time; "we all know they wander, but do we need to know how far – or have neighbouring keepers' gloat when they discover that one of your carefully reared and released birds has been shot on their estate and been added to their bag?" He might well have had a point!

July – a prelude to autumn
1st July 2009

July is a strange month. It is of very little interest to ferreters, can produce some poor days for the fly fisherman, and is the month in which most pheasants are released. Given good weather, it's an excellent month to rear a litter of puppies and an ideal time to host a sporting get-together. It is, of course, also the month when all British field sports have the focal point of the annual Game Fair. At what should, weather permitting, be the height of summer, it is difficult to believe that the grouse shooting season is only seven weeks away. Closely followed by the opening of the partridge shooting season and, a month after that, the chance of an early pheasant or two, July has, in my mind at least, always been linked to the fact that there is now likely to be no respite for the gamekeeping fraternity for the next few months.

Memories of my July days on the grouse moor include the last minute checking of butts in order to ensure that the sheep – which delight in using them as shelters – haven't rubbed and disturbed any of the stones. All of ours were permanent circular structures, and it might also have been necessary at this time to replace some of the heather or whinberry turf that topped off the butt and helped prevent guns from being damaged when laid there in readiness for the drive to begin. Sheep droppings also needed clearing from inside the butts and the little primitive drains that ensured the floor never flooded would often require a bit of a poke with a walking stick. Being the youngest in a team of five keepers, it also always seemed to be my job to sweep out the shooting lodge; make flags for the flankers and also to construct the folding wooden markers that were strategically placed by the loaders on either "wing" of the butt in order to ensure that there could be no dangerous shooting down the line.

On the lowground shoot, July is of course, a very busy time indeed. Not only are there last minute checks to be made to the release pens prior to taking the first poults out, but it is also important to make sure that there is no long grass or vegetation immediately surrounding the pen. Foxes soon become very adept at picking up birds in thick cover, and cutting around the immediate area will prevent losses from predation as the birds first come down from roost. It may not be possible to cut certain headlands if the farm is involved in a particular government grant scheme but, conversely, some meadow grass will require topping to qualify for other payments, and perhaps the farmer could be persuaded to cut this prior to your young pheasants finding their way out of the release pens.

There is usually a point this month when the shoot that rears its own birds from day old, has birds in the release pen and also some on the rearing field. Both require equal attention and it is not always easy to get into any sort of feeding routine. There is also sometimes the need to clear the rearing field of sheds and sections straight away – the latter quite often being needed elsewhere on the shoot in order to release partridges at suitable sites.

Incidentally, on shoots where there are still some of last year's partridges around but they have no offspring of their own, advantage can be taken of the fact that these old birds will readily adopt coveys of hand-reared chicks. The earlier this is arranged the better: partridge poults are placed in their holding unit somewhere near to where adult birds have been regularly seen, and as soon as they have been noticed hanging around the pen for a few days, the young birds can be carefully liberated.

Dry weather and the fact that harvesting this month will leave stubble, normally means that it is relatively easy to get around the shoot with whatever transport is available. Amongst all the other jobs then, it might be an idea to take advantage of this fact and get out as many hoppers and straw bales as possible to the various feeding points that may be unreachable later in the year. The stubble and dry fields also means that it's a good time to catch up with a bit of night-shooting to cull the rabbits on behalf of the farmer, or to sort out a few three-quarter grown fox cubs on behalf of yourself!

Lamping at night with a shotgun or rifle is a good way of catching up with foxes and rabbits and is permissible, provided that it is carried out

Combining allows the opportunity for night-shooting in Britain, but not in France where such things are illegal.

by either the occupier of the land or a person authorized by him. If you are a shooting tenant, probably the most practical and simplest proof of permission is in the form of a written note or letter. This should include the identity of the holder, the date, the ground/area of land covered, the signature of the occupier and what form of firearms may be used. Simple common courtesy says that you make a point of telling any immediate neighbours that you are out, especially if they have young children who may be disturbed, also that you avoid areas where livestock is grazing and that you finish as early as is practicable. It is also essential that you let your local police authority know what you are doing if you wish to avoid being chased across a stubble field by a flashing blue light!

PREDATOR CONTROL

A brood or two of wild pheasants or partridge are arguably more important to the small shoot than they are on the commercial estate. On the very small shoot where few if any birds are released, they could make a huge difference. The old books' talk of stoats and weasels being a problem with nesting birds but it is undoubtedly the magpies and crows that take most eggs and newly-hatched chicks and there is a continual need to try and control their numbers.

Where professional keepers have the advantage over "amateurs" is that, being on the ground all the time, they can get to grips with predator control in a more efficient way than can the "part-timer" or D.I.Y. syndicate member who rarely has such luxury due to the fact they need to earn a wage elsewhere!

Not being around all the time, it can often be difficult to check traps and snares at the right time of day – and keep within legalities with regard to the amount of times they should be checked. As with a feeding rota during the winter whereby shoot members take a weekly or morning/evening shift, it might, however, be possible to employ similar methods so that this all-important task is done efficiently whilst still managing to conform to government legislation.

As far as the situation in the UK is concerned, there is plenty of relevant information on the BASC, National Gamekeepers' Organisation and Countryside Alliance websites. In France, things can, at times, be very different indeed and some methods that would have you locked up in Britain are legal, permissible and quite acceptable!

Frightening figures
25th April 2012

I've recently been struggling to read a French report on the subject which neighbour Maurice had been sent from his local shooting organisation and in which he thought I might be interested. When it came to the subject of predation on grey partridges, the research work of the Game and Conservation Wildlife Trust (GCWT) gets a very honourable mention – much of which focused on the fact that foxes, corvids and stoats were likely to be the main problem facing any gamekeeper wanting to preserve his wild stocks of such birds.

Not to be outdone by the GCWT, the "Office national de la chasse et de la faune sauvage" (ONCFS) have conducted a great deal of research into the welfare and predation of red-leg partridges over here. As a result of fitting radio-trackers and CCTV cameras in areas where partridges are known to frequent, it seems that wild bird numbers in the middle of the country have reduced since the last study was carried out in

1989. Somewhat alarmingly, around 40 percent of springtime nests are lost through predation, mainly from foxes, magpies, stoats, weasels and polecats. To have any chance of breeding success, trapping is therefore, essential.

Much the same conclusion was reached when it came to pheasants – although, for some reason, the report centred on studies made in America rather than here in France. As far as predation on rabbits and hares was concerned, rather more national research has been carried out – although the dossier does rather labour on one particular project carried out in Switzerland between 2004-2006 in which it seems foxes and feral cats were the main culprits.

Protecting the poacher
16th September 2009

There seems to be some confusion in France as to what is regarded as a predator or vermin and although members of various anti-hunting groups may well consider those of us who hunt, shoot and fish as being vermin, there is a clear list of animals and birds that have the legal status of being "harmful" or "nuisibles". The list includes magpies, crows, jays, weasels and foxes; or at least it did at one time, but now things are not so clear cut.

In December 2002, certain species such as beech, stone and pine martens and weasels became protected by government law. After much debate, they were then reinstated to the "nuisibles" list until, in December 2008, a ministerial decree put them back in the "protected" column. This action resulted in the prefectures of many departments having to issue notification to anyone remotely involved in shooting and gamekeeping that the likes of magpies, rooks, carrion crows, starlings, weasels and martens cannot now be trapped or shot outside the authorised shooting seasons. The animal rights organization, ASPAS claim responsibility for this about face and cite their campaigning in accordance with an administrative court ruling as being "significant".

At the time, ASPAS issued a statement in respect of the actual damage that the likes of martens, stoats and weasels do, part of which stated that: "The vacillation of the legal status in any case demonstrates the lack of biological basis of the concept of 'harmful'. All scientific studies in Europe show that the diet of mustelids is not harmful to biodiversity or to farms. Instead, these large consumers of rodents are very useful for agriculture and forestry." Whilst one cannot deny that they do capture and kill rats and mice, I wonder which way the scientists and conservationists were looking when it comes to observing just how many other species (gamebirds included) also feature in their diet. There appears to be a curious discrepancy between the world of research and biological reality!

I recently read a very interesting French article written by a certain Marie-Claude Vadrot who claimed that whilst he was not a "hunter", neither was he an opponent of hunting "when practiced in accordance with the laws, French or European, and ethics appropriate to the 21st Century." Several very balanced points were made in the piece, not least of which was the undeniable fact that in some places game has become so abundant

Poachers – a protected species?!

that it calls into question the natural regeneration of woodland and flora by eating shrubs and devastating crops. Marie-Claude Vadrot also had an opinion on the numbers of game shot. He claimed, quite rightly in my opinion, that game shooters who scour the countryside in the company of friends and dogs they love and then eat what they manage to kill, show knowledge and respect for their natural environment. However, they are, according to him, "no longer the majority, far from it."

Perhaps of most interest however, were Vadrot's thoughts on poachers and, rather than risk losing the actual context by apprising his words, I quote his final paragraph in full: "Admiration for those who hunt because they can sniff the wind, find minute traces, guess the habits of animals, leads to another thought: I am for the protection of the true poacher; not for those that shoot at anything that moves whilst perched on a 4 x 4 and sell their ill-gotten gains for profit, but for those who have the talent to know intimately where he can place his trap or snare. In my mind, the last poachers are a species to protect, just as the wolf, bear, lynx, wild cat, genet, otter, marten and weasel."

Rats on the shoot
18th June 2008

I have a phobia about rats – so much so that I come over "all unnecessary" if I so much as see a photo of one. As you might imagine, such a handicap doesn't help me much when, as a country living boy, rats are common place. Thankfully, despite a chicken run, bird table and, until recently, an aviary, it is rare to see a rat around "Le Malineau", but in my keeping days, they were a regular sight, despite the fact that I kept a regular supply of poison around the feed sheds, rearing fields and woodland feed tracks. They have, I must admit, given me some exciting sport with terriers and for those like me who have a fear of them, there is nothing more adrenalin and hair-sticking-up-on-the-back-of-your-neck inducing, than to be in a confined space when rats attempt to scramble up the wall whilst pursued by a small pack of motley terriers. Generally however, the most efficient way of ridding a place of rats is by poison.

There are so many types on the market that it is difficult to know which to choose. Personally, I prefer to use either the waxed blocks or the sort that you lay as bait whilst still in a plastic sachet. Knowing the rat's propensity to chew anything plastic, the manufacturer's idea is that the poison will remain unaffected by damp, staying fresh until it is gnawed upon.

Whenever the subject of rat poison is discussed, there are always those who claim that rats have become immune to the anti-coagulant type of poison such as *Warfarin*. One theory is that they have not in fact, become immune, more that some have survived ingesting small doses and as a consequence, become "bait-shy". It is for this reason that it is important to ensure that there is always a sufficient supply of poison once a baiting programme has begun. It may also pay to periodically change the type of poison being used.

As with most things, it is easier to prevent an invasion of rats onto your shoot and around your poultry houses and kennels than it is to eradicate them once they have set up home. Make every effort to prevent their access by laying down concrete floors or, alternatively, in the case of hen houses and the like, raise the floors so that there is no security for them underneath. Place gratings on drains and small mesh wire over any openings. Rats will find it easier to enter a building if the walls are covered in ivy or similar vegetation and will use it as a ladder in order to enter a building from under the eaves.

Keep a constant look-out for signs of rats and remember the old adage, "If you see droppings, you've got a rat. If you see a rat hole you've got a family of 'em. If you hear rats at night, you've several families. And if you see rats during the day – run ..." Actually, I just made the last bit up, but it's what I do!

A Larsen at "Le Malineau"
16th March 2011

Because we had a more than usual amount of rain last month, it seems that the expression "February Fill-dyke" might apply equally here in France as it traditionally does in Britain, and the ditches and streams are indeed full. This is obviously good news for ducks as I've seen many a pair fly up out of secluded narrow waterways whilst out for a walk with the dog. In fact I saw signs of a duck nest just a matter of days ago. I might have missed it were it not for the tell-tale downy breast feathers with which the female tends to cover her nest whilst off feeding. If I could see it, it's a pretty safe bet that magpies and crows will and, positioned where it is, I don't give much for its chances.

We have a Larsen trap here at "Le Malineau" and are moderately successful in catching a few magpies each spring and early summer. The French tend to use circular weld-mesh traps rather than Larsens and so the "chasse" members were very interested when I first showed it to them. In fact one of them went away and built his own which he now uses on the perimeter of his chicken run.

As many will know, the siting of such a trap is very important and I have, on several occasions, had one set at one side of a hedge and had no luck but just as soon as I relocated it a few yards to the other side, have caught magpies within hours. However, the positioning of our house and land here seems perfect so I leave the Larsen in the same place each season and always manage to pick up corvids as they fly from the corner of the wood to our hedge-line of tall "look-out" trees.

When we first arrived, my biggest problem was obtaining a live magpie

A Larsen trap is perhaps the most effective method of corvid control on any side of the Channel. (Photo: Philip Watts)

to act as decoy. At the time, I didn't know anyone locally except for neighbour Maurice and even he, with all his contacts, was unable to help. In the end, I opted to use a plastic decoy bought from the local gunshop and whilst it obviously doesn't have the advantage of noise and movement, it generally entices a magpie into the trap eventually and I then use that one as decoy for the remainder of the time that the trap is in use.

This year I caught my first magpie within a day of setting the trap and he in turn has since lured another five. If I can catch a similar amount in the next few weeks, that will be my average for the season. Ten isn't many when one sees just how prolific magpie numbers are in the area, but if I only ever caught one, it is one less to do damage to wild game and song bird stocks.

Rook pie for supper
25th April 2012

At this time of year, most keepers and shoot managers have all their tunnel traps and Larsen traps in action. As yet, so far at "Le Malineau", I've caught but one magpie in the Larsen; nonetheless, if things compare to other years, I will hopefully increase the tally in the next couple of weeks or so. It's the magpies and crows I really want to keep down as, although I'm obviously no longer actively involved in professional gamekeeping, reducing their numbers will help the wild pheasant and partridge stocks – and the song birds, of which I'm rather fond.

Even as far back as the 16th Century, the authorities of the time recognised the fact that corvids of any description, but particularly rooks and crows, were detrimental to game birds; a nuisance around buildings by dint of the fact that they had a tendency to pull out the thatch of cottages and barns, and to farmer's crops. A Parliamentary Act of 1533 decreed that every parish must keep nets for catching rooks and, in addition, if permission had been asked for and refused, anyone was entitled to ignore that fact and enter land in order to destroy rooks without then becoming liable for damages to trespass. Of course we now realise that rooks probably do more good than harm as far as agriculture is concerned due to the fact that they pull out leather-jackets and other harmful grubs from the soil.

Nevertheless, there has always been a tradition of shooting young rooks towards the middle of next month. Originally, 12th May was the official rook-shooting day in most parts of the countryside and was chosen because it was the time when the majority of the year's offspring were leaving the nest. Known as "branchers", they were easy to shoot and the meat was very tender, making a pie a popular meal, especially for the poor and latterly during the Second World War when meat was very scarce. It is, however, only the breasts and top part of the thighs that are edible, and the back and skin meat is bitter and black. They must, therefore, be skinned and carefully sorted before being cooked.

Whether they still do I'm unsure but, certainly at one time, The King's Arms at Didmarton in Gloucestershire used to hold an annual Rook Supper. This particular venue apparently came about as the result of a ready supply of rook meat being supplied by gamekeepers employed on a neighbouring estate. If it is still being held, it's probably as good a place as any to go and taste rook pie if you don't fancy the idea of doing it yourself!

Feral cats and Radio 4
27th June 2012

As I write, I can see the resident "Le Malineau" wren dashing in and out of its usual nesting spot in the low wall in the garden and I'm well aware of a blackbird sitting on a nest of eggs in the vine growing over the kitchen door. When I go and make myself a coffee (as I will in a very short while!), I know that, as I look out of the window waiting for the kettle to boil, I shall be able to watch a pair of tits busily bringing feed to their fledglings which hatched safe and sound in a small gap in the house wall.

Unlike many of the farms and houses in the neighbourhood, "Le Malineau" is a cat-free zone and that must go a long way towards ensuring the safety of, not only song birds, but also any game bird chicks that do manage to hatch off in the nearby hedgerows. Although I'm not a cat person, I don't actually dislike them, I am, however, well aware of what damage they can cause.

Over the years, I (along with most other keepers, I suspect) have come across several domestic cats that have gone feral and, because of their lack of fear of humans and their supreme ability to climb wooden posts, over-hanging tree branches, and even crawl under a strand of electric fence and squeeze through an anti-fox grid, have sometimes managed to enter a release pen. Whilst, apart from the first few nights when pheasant poults tend to jug on the ground rather than go up to roost, they might not kill many, their presence certainly un-nerves the birds and prevents them from exploring the pen, feeding and generally behaving in a natural manner. The "pinking" alarm call of a blackbird is a good indicator that something is wrong in a release pen and all song birds will warn of a cat in the vicinity: signs of other possible predators are not, however, always as easy to detect.

Although it is definitely more time-consuming, I've always favoured hand-feeding pheasants over hopper feeding – especially in the release pen. It gives ample opportunity to check birds for signs of disease or discontent and, if they are suddenly reluctant to come out onto the feed ride and prefer instead to stay skulking in the undergrowth, there's a very good chance that a sparrowhawk has been working the ride. There is, of course, nothing one can do to eradicate the problem and I'd like to think that no modern-thinking keeper would ever be tempted into taking the law into their own hands. There are though, certain measures that might

In order to deter birds of prey around the release pen, some ideas worth experimenting with include strips of silver foil and even old CD discs left spinning on a thread.

just act as a deterrent until the poults are old enough not to be troubled by such activity.

Some ideas worth experimenting with include strips of silver foil and even old CD discs left spinning on a thread in the hope that the sudden flash as the light catches them might cause sparrowhawks to fly off in alarm. Flashing amber road-lights have also been put to good use at night to protect newly released pheasants from being harassed by tawny owls. There are even those who advocate leaving a radio tuned to a speaking station in the hope that the sound of human voices might put off both birds of prey and foxes – in fact, it was only recently that I heard of a UK nature reserve who are now using radios tuned into BBC Radio 4 as a means of keeping foxes away from ground-nesting birds.

5

Gundogs
and Running Dogs

I'VE been lucky with my dogs in that I've tended to "gel" with most of them – and them with me. The majority have been spaniels and, when I started my gamekeeping career, they were English Springer's. Headstrong though they may generally thought to be, I seemed to "click" with all but one – and that was one I bought as an adult rather than a pup or youngster. Yet bizarrely, its litter sister I knew well worked brilliantly for its owner and it was that fact which tempted me to buy the dog when it suddenly became available. Maybe the fact that it was "suddenly" available should have set warning bells ringing in my head!

Peter Moxon, the renowned gun-dog trainer and well-known for being a "cocker knocker", did nothing to prevent me from buying a young Cocker pup from a neighbouring gamekeeper – and it was the best move, dog-wise, that I ever made. It was from Hedley Millington's Nancarrow bloodline and she and Merlin (an ESS) were undoubtedly the two easiest and most biddable spaniels it's ever been my pleasure to train. Merlin caused more than one person to suggest that I worked him by either an invisible string or remote control and Alice, the Cocker, always proved perfect in the beating line right up until the last few yards of the drive when she would break rank and rush out to pick up a fallen bird. Her reliability in doing so was such that, when my employer gave his start of the day safety speech and briefing, he eventually stopped saying "the end of the drive is signalled by a whistle" and instead, told his guests that, "you'll know the drive is over when a black spaniel appears and runs the length of the line!"

I bred some lovely pups from Alice and all worked well for me and other owners of the subsequent litters. Yet, despite following very close pedigree bloodlines, when I bought, from an outsider, a Cocker dog of similar ilk, he and I really did not "gel" and I eventually sold him on as a family pet where he proved brilliant at agility tests and subsequently went on to win many competitions.

I had a very brief flirtation with Labradors. In my late 20's, I thought I'd buy a lovely little black bitch from a working litter. Perfect in every way, although she was happy to work for me, I got no enjoyment whatsoever from working with her. Sold to the wife of a neighbouring gamekeeper however, the two of them "gelled" perfectly. A decade later I bought a part-trained Labrador dog which, like the bitch beforehand, was kind and biddable – and yet there was something "missing" in our relationship. The son of our game dealer took him on – and won several gundog tests and field trials. The fact that I cannot even remember the names of these two Labs says much about me and nothing about them. I can, however, remember the names of my various terriers.

At the age of 12 and, unbeknown to my parents as I kept him at a friend's family farm for a few months before I told them I was its owner, my first ever was Nick, a Jack Russell x Chihuahua. The fact that his parents ever got it together was, presumably a mistake yet he was a perfect ratting and rabbiting dog. Once my parents could see the route I was taking, Nick was allowed home – and was, not all that long afterwards, joined by Penny, the most perfect looking wire-haired, straight-legged Jack Russell so like the drawings of the original Trump, it was unbelievable.

She and I spent all our free time together and, all credit to my father, he would take the two of us to various working terrier shows organised by the hunts where, without exception, Penny would come somewhere in the top three. Although we most definitely "gelled", the terrier and owner relationship was sadly curtailed on the day that Penny broke from her kennel and was shot by a neighbouring free-range poultry farmer in the (mistaken) belief that it was her who had previously killed some of his geese.

Once Penny and Nick had gone and my teenage gamekeepering training was secured, it was time for Jasper, my first ever Springer. After that, though, alongside the spaniels (and short-lived flirtations with Labradors!), there was always the opportunity and need for terriers. In my youth I had been out on Sunday morning forays with the local hunt and seen them dig out foxes and badgers with Lakeland terriers. I'd even been up to the Lakes several times to watch the Fell packs and seen how they had used local terriers to bolt the fox – and yet I'd never had the inclination towards a Fell terrier. Perhaps I'd realised, even at that early stage, they and I would not "gel".

Eventually employed as a keeper in the south of England – and needing to keep the estate free of foxes that could be bolted from enlarged rabbit holes or very shallow earths – I purchased "Gyp", a short-legged, smooth-coated "Russell". He was certainly from good stock and worked well (and sensibly) when up against a fox but, like the Labradors, he and I never really developed that all-important "close bond".

Nettle, on the other hand, was very different and was the first dog I'd ever had in the house rather than a kennel. Although quite close in appearance to Penny, she was a superb ratter, but not much good for her intended purpose of foxing. By that time, however, I was married and had children and she was very definitely an all-round family favourite!

Jasper – my first ever spaniel.

How much is that doggy in the window?
17th October 2005

I can understand the current prices being paid in Britain for well-bred working dogs whether they are terriers, sight hounds or gundogs, but I cannot for the life of me see why less useful breeds are so expensive. On my recent trip back to England I learned of a litter of "Labradoodles" – apparently the latest must-have fashion item – being sold for £800 each. Why would anyone want to pay so much for what is, by any other name, merely a cross-breed?

Obviously, there are exceptions that prove the rule, lurchers for instance, have evolved over the years in order to combine the best of two (or more) breeds, but generally a cross-bred working dog is, in my opinion, a bad idea. In my gamekeeping days I heard frequently of deliberate crosses between Labradors and spaniels and the like which were being bred in the fond hope that the resultant puppy would contain the best genes of both breeds. Enquiring after the litter at a later stage, it seemed that they were just as likely to incorporate the worst aspects of the parents.

As to prices for dogs in France: they seem to have remained pretty constant for the last couple of years or so. In a magazine I have in front of me I see that I could, if I were so minded, buy a 12-week-old German shorthaired pointer for 600 euros or a Labrador, apparently bred from a strain that originated on an English shooting estate, for 500 euros. A four-year-old terrier is for sale for 300 euros, due only to the death of the owner, but of "Labradoodles" I can see no mention!

Maurice has just added two beagle pups to his kennel of shooting dogs. I know that because they appeared in our garden the other day with their owner in hot pursuit. A typical Frenchman, he is blessed with an impressive stomach gained over years of serious eating and drinking and is certainly not cut out to be chasing puppies around the countryside in hot weather! Sweat was dripping from his brow, eventually finding its way into his impressive moustache and so, once we'd caught the errant puppies, it was only neighbourly to offer him a drink. As Maurice fervently believes that water is for washing in, there was no point in offering anything other than a glass of our local Rosé.

Interested in why the French sportsman favours hounds equally as much as the more traditional types of gundog, I asked the question but,

Maurice's two new beagles come to visit!

other than the fact that they are useful for following up a wounded deer or boar, failed to get a real answer as to why they were also used by those who only ever shoot small game. That they are in great demand is evidenced by the prices charged – a beagle puppy can, according to Maurice, cost around 500 euros whilst a hound that is already trained to "own" a blood scent may command a selling price of anywhere between 1,000-1,500 euros.

Confined to barracks
23rd March 2011

Dogs need exercise – elementary one might think, but, whereas most UK sporting dog owners tend to keep their animals in a reasonably fit condition throughout the "close season", from what I've observed over the years, the French sportsman does not.

Writing this on a Sunday morning, it's sad to think that, in many of the rural houses around me, there are sporting dogs shut in their kennels which would, as I write, normally have been getting their exercise hunting up the hedgerows and across the fields. Now, with the shooting season finished, their Sundays will be very different. For the foreseeable future, the best most of them can expect is to be let out into the garden for a few minutes each day; others will quite literally, be confined to barracks until the season starts again in September. Apart from being fed and cleaned out, all they have to look forward to is the glimpse of someone coming up the garden path or passing by on the lane – which is no way to keep an animal physically exercised and mentally stimulated.

The strange thing is that these are not mongrel dogs, but pure-breeds which will have cost their owners quite a few euros to purchase. Just looking through the classified adverts in this month's *Le Chasseur Français* magazine shows that a trained 14-month-old German shorthaired pointer will set someone back 1,400 euros, a 10-month working beagle, 1,100 euros, and a teckel pup 350 euros.

Gundog trainers abound in France and it is not just the wealthy Guns who send their dogs to "school" as might be the case in Britain. So there is also the distinct possibility that some of the local "chasseurs" will have spent good money on the services of a trainer in addition to the initial cost of a dog. None of which makes any sense at all.

As we all know, dogs need regular exercise to keep "ticking over" and their minds stimulated by some dummy work or general basic re-training over the following months. It would be foolish, not to say cruel, just to lock them away for the summer as one might a shotgun. Of course, there are exceptions and some French sportsmen and women who own HPR, pointer and setter breeds compete in working tests between now and September. In fact, like the UK game fairs, there are often such competitions attached to the various "fêtes de la chasse" held throughout France during June, July and August. There is, I must admit, not a lot better than being a spectator at one of these events when you can sit under the shade of a tree with a beer in hand and just watch the world go by!

Walking the dog
10th April 2013

I like the fact that, here in France, none of the local farmers and viticulturalists object to my walking the dog more or less where I like across their land during our long morning jaunts. Generally, throughout France, there are no restrictions on walking in the forests – provided of course that they are not marked up as "private", or there is no temporary notification advising that shooting or tree work is in progress. There may, however, be restrictions on certain protected sites such as in a "parc national".

Things are, nevertheless, a little different when it comes to this time of year as a piece of French legislation (which has been in place since 1955) prevents anyone walking along wood and forest tracks between the period April 15 – June 30 without having their dog on a lead. The reason behind this edict is that, during this time, wild ground nesting birds and various animals are at their most vulnerable due to it being their optimum breeding season. There is much merit in this thinking, but, in my opinion, it is far more important that all dogs are reasonably controlled when off the lead and not allowed to run riot at any time of the year.

During my time as a gamekeeper in both North Yorkshire and southern England, I lost count of the number of times I encountered dog-walkers (both on and off public footpaths) whose dogs were running around uncontrollably and when asked politely to bring their dog to heel, responded by saying, "but they're not doing any harm … they're just having a bit of fun and not hurting anything." Sometimes it was possible to explain that they might easily disturb ground-nesting birds, or, that young pheasants and partridges had recently been released in that area: more often than not, though, my reasoned arguments would be met with resentment and, at best, a surly agreement to put the dog on a lead. In the worse case scenario, my request would be totally ignored and the walker march on: but in both, I know that the dog would have been allowed to continue exactly as before once it and its owner was out of sight.

Any disturbance to nesting game at this time of year is bad enough, but it can obviously have a far more telling effect on wild bird shoots and, in particular, grouse moors where, apart from heather burning and predator control, the keeper can do no more than hope that the weather is kind during the nesting season – and that sitting females are not troubled as a result of walkers and their dogs exercising their "right to roam".

Pointing the way
4th June 2008

Perhaps it's because there are not as many "big" shoots around us in France as there are in England, but whatever the reason, I've noticed since being here that French-bred spaniels of any type are more inclined to go on point just before flushing game than they are in the UK. The connection between the two observations is that if a spaniel, or any dog for that matter, pointed every time they winded game and the beating line was held up for them, it would take all day just to do one drive on some of the larger British shoots!

From talking to spaniel owners, it appears that they do not train their dogs to go on point; it is just something that has evolved over many generations – it is certainly very useful, as it gives the shooting handler precious extra time in which to line themselves up for the most advantageous shot. Rough shooting is, of course, very different to the driven shoot and a dog which points is a very useful asset in places where game is widely spread and every bird has to be worked for. That is very much the case with "commune" shooting and probably explains why Maurice and his cronies are accompanied by HPR breeds as well as Labradors, spaniels and hounds. Actually training the HPR breeds to point is another matter entirely. Obviously, because of the nature of their breeding, it is far more natural for any of these types to point instinctively, but this inherited ability is enhanced by French trainers when the puppies are very young. Some time ago, I visited a professional trainer and was fascinated to see how he encouraged this very desirable attribute.

A Braque du Bourbonnais "on point".

Taking the puppies out into a paddock behind the kennels, he gently swung a light lure made of wing feathers at the end of a short piece of light cord attached to a fairly robust fishing rod – don't try this with your best split-cane Hardy – over the heads of the pups. Naturally, they were very interested in what was going on and began chasing the lure as it passed over them. After a few minutes, the trainer gently dropped the lure to the ground and at first the puppies rushed up to it in order to take a better look. After a couple more swings, the next time the lure was dropped to the ground every single one of the litter ran towards it, but instead of trying to grab it as you might expect them to do, stopped short and went on a perfect "point".

Such training, so the trainer assured me, worked with every litter of puppies he had ever bred – it would be interesting to see whether the same results could be achieved with a litter of spaniels.

Exuberance at a French working test
15th November 2006

In France, all pure-bred puppies receive a three-generation pedigree at the time of sale. To receive a full five-generation pedigree and also to be eligible for registration with the Société Centrale Canine (the French equivalent of the Kennel Club), any working gundog must be assessed by an official "confirmateur" appointed by the SCC before it can be graded as either "excellent", "very good" or "good". Once this has been completed, its subsequent rating will dictate its desirability as a breeding bitch or stud dog, as well as its future eligibility for working tests and field trials.

A couple of months ago, my wife and I were invited to an open working test for hunt/point/retrieve breeds and as a result, spent a glorious autumn afternoon watching some lovely-looking young dogs as they competed over a mixture of stubble and flat water meadows. Each group of dogs had their own designated area over which to hunt, but even so, the contestants that had been drawn last in their particular group had the added problem of foiled scenting from the dogs and handlers that had run earlier.

In a French working test of this nature, the dogs are expected to hunt up to a "dizzied" quail and then hold a strong point until the judge kicks up the bird and a blank firing pistol is shot. From what we were told by our hosts, the judge is looking for hunting drive and passion, a proper point, no fear of gunshot and a lack of aggressiveness towards people or other dogs. Steadiness to flush is not expected at this stage.

Having watched several similar tests in the UK, it was immediately apparent that there is a significant difference in the training methods between France and Great Britain – whereas in the UK, all gundog handlers tend to introduce discipline and control early in a puppy's life, the French try not to curtail their dog's natural ability. Whether or not the examples my wife and I watched were accurate representatives of this philosophy, it did appear that the particular dogs we saw had a tendency to ignore all commands whether whistled or shouted, and seemed on occasions to hunt purely for themselves.

Most dogs found a bird within a reasonable time span, although there did not appear to be a limit imposed and, even though some dogs that failed to quarter up to their quarry were eventually asked to withdraw, most eventually pointed, even if they did not hold the point for long. Some were almost on top of the bird when they did so, but we noticed that several only got to about a yard from the quail before coming up on point. Almost every dog chased the bird for some distance when it was kicked up, and some even caught them, in contrast to pointing breeds in the UK which seem, from my admittedly very limited experience, to be steadier in their quartering, more under their handler's control and hold the point for a longer period of time.

In a trance
4th June 2008

I don't know who it was who first discovered the practice of "dizzying" quail or any other type of game bird nor what were their reasons for doing so, but it can be quite useful when training all types of gundog. In the past I've used this trick practically as well as to amuse my children when they were small.

The basic method is to place the bird's head under its wing; cradle its body in both hands and gently rock your hands back and forth. In a very short space of time the bird appears to be in a trance and it can be gently laid on the ground where it will remain quietly until being "kicked" up by the handler, at which stage they suddenly come back to "normal" and fly off. In various French working tests I've watched the stewards use similar methods but instead of rocking the bird, they've held it in one hand, extended their arm and whirled it round in a circular motion.

Many years ago, I was responsible for organizing a working test demonstration at a country show and borrowed a neighbour's pigeons which I used like the French use their quail in order to show the pointing ability of a team of English setters. I dare not use the pigeons in the same way for the spaniels in case an over-enthusiastic one caught what were quite expensive racing birds! For them, I constructed a small cage with a trap door that could be lifted from a distance by means of a long piece of string.

On another occasion, I had a young Springer spaniel that I just could not get to watch my hands when trying to teach it quartering. The evening before I was due to take 1,000 pheasant poults to wood, I caught up half a dozen and let all bar one go in the corner of an empty release pen. I dizzied the one remaining, hunted the spaniel through all the parts of the pen that contained no scent and then really concentrated the dog on quartering the ground where the poults had been released. By now the spaniel was taking note of my hand movements and, as he came up on the dizzied bird, he learned what he was hunting for and I made a great fuss of him when the young pheasant ran off. I did the same again in a couple more pens over the next few days, at the end of which time; the puppy seemed more than happy to hunt in whichever direction I sent him.

Giving in to temptation
8th October 2008

I have just been offered two Weimaraners, "free to a good home", by the owner of a local bar, but I shall not be taking up the offer. Apparently, they are litter brother and sister, bred in France and are being re-homed because they are unmanageable. Poor dogs, they are now two years old and, apart from the times they have escaped from their run and disappeared over the horizon, have had no exercise or indeed, any time and effort spent on them. No wonder they are unmanageable and will, unless now taken on by someone with an understanding of canine behaviour and a fair degree of patience, presumably continue in the same way and will never be any good either on or off the shooting field.

To even a well-trained dog, a sudden flush of birds, or the increasingly exciting build-up of scent as game runs forward in the drive on a shooting day, can sometimes prove an overwhelming temptation to the dog and a headache for the keeper or person in charge of the beating line. Occasionally, in a game crop, for example, it may not be the dog's fault because they perhaps cannot hear the instructions of their handler due to the noise of kale leaves or dried-out maize stems bashing about their ears. But, no matter what the situation, there is very little point in the keeper getting upset and shouting abuse – which may cause even more birds to flush. The owner of the errant animal will, in all probability, be doing enough shouting and whistling anyway and any extra noise will do no good whatsoever. Easier said than done of course, and I have not been without blame on such occasions during my own gamekeeping days!

In heavy woodland where visibility is poor, an unruly or temporarily out-of-control dog can still prove disastrous. If, for instance, a particular wood is being relied upon to produce a steady stream of high-flying pheasants and a beater's dog rushes forward after a rabbit, there is the very strong possibility that it will come up against and flush all the birds that have been carefully driven to a point from which they can best be shown and the drive will be over in seconds with very little to show for it.

Another part of the day at which dogs may go off to do their own thing is between drives. The handler's attention is often elsewhere as he or she talks to a fellow beater and there is the excitement of other dogs milling around. In such a situation, a dog can get disorientated, or take advantage of the circumstances in order to prematurely start the next drive. So, unless your dog is without question, and to use an equine term, totally "bombproof", never feel that it is beneath your dignity or a sign of a badly trained dog, to keep yours on a lead at such times.

Travelling in style
28th September 2011

Looking at how people transport their dogs to and from the shoot during the winter months, there appears to be some good, well designed travel boxes and cages on the market at the moment. Professional and semi-professional gundog handlers and trainers who do a lot of picking-up and possibly also give demonstrations at the various game fairs held during the summer months may even have the luxury of a purpose-built trailer

– which, I would guess, be beyond the means of most of us unless it's possible to do as they do and find a generous sponsor.

Here in France, however, it seems that most of the commune chasse members use such trailers, albeit somewhat smaller than the ones I've just been mentioning. Quite why, I've no idea as most of the cars that tow them seem as if they've been lucky to pass their "controle technique" (the French equivalent of an MOT) and half a dozen dogs careering around the interior wouldn't make a lot of difference.

Hounds, particularly beagles, have been traditionally taken to UK meets in the back of a trailer, although having said that, I can think of several packs which use a transit type van in which to transport them. Larger hounds from the mounted packs often travel to the meet in a partitioned part of a horse box. Some of these are quite cleverly designed in tiers with a "basement" and "first-floor level" in order to make the optimum use of space available. It obviously makes a great deal of financial and economic sense to be able to get both horses for the hunt staff and the hounds all to the same place in one vehicle.

Luxury travel as far as this particular trailer's occupants are concerned!

All dog trailers or boxes fitted into the back of an open pick-up need to conform to certain criteria when it comes to creature comforts and legalities. Boxes must be securely fixed to prevent them from sliding about, and both trailers and boxes must have adequate ventilation which will not suck in exhaust fumes. If they've been made specifically for the job in mind, all should be well as far as insulation is concerned, but it should be remembered that, despite the best efforts of some very clever designers, they can very quickly get hot and should always be parked up under shade. Shade and heat is not generally a problem during the shooting season, but if competing in working tests or giving demonstrations during the summer months, it might well be.

Cages or boxes that fit inside the car need to be big enough to ensure that a dog can stand up, sit down and turn round comfortably. If you're travelling with more than one dog, the cage ought to be partitioned because if a disagreement occurs, there could be some serious injuries inflicted before it is possible for you to pull off the road in order to sort things out. Fortunately, most gundog breeds are pretty kind to one another – you only have to see them piled on top of one another in the average beater's trailer to see that – but even so, it's a risk probably not worth taking.

It's got bells on …
12th October 2011

In certain parts of France, especially wooded areas where woodcock are known to frequent, pointing and setting dogs and a few steady spaniels have always been fitted with a bell to their collar. Not only does the bell allow the owner to have a rough idea as to where his dog is at most times, when the noise stops, there's a good chance that the animal has gone "on point", giving him a few important moments to ready himself before the bird or beast flushes from cover.

However, the traditional bell is being increasingly usurped in favour of an electronic collar which works in the same way as does the "sat-nav" in your car. With a short aerial attached to a collar similar to that used on locators fitted to ferrets or terriers, modern technology certainly does not have the same visual charm as the old-fashioned, deep-sounding bell.

There seems to be a more serious problem though – that of non-conformity – and the national agency that deals with monitoring radio licences and air frequencies in France has, for some reason, decided that one particular model should be made illegal. The Garmin Astro 220/ DC40, made specifically for hunting dogs, and distributed in France by a company called "New Hunting Technologies", has just been banned. Not only has it been banned, there are amazingly serious repercussions for anyone discovered using it. A top fine of 30,000 euros or up to six months in prison has been mentioned. There can be no doubt that the traditional bell is a far more appealing option!

A bell around the neck of a pointer or setter is the traditional way of locating one's dog in the woodlands of France.

Rag and rabbit chasing
28th February 2009

I'm probably not telling a single reader what they don't already know when I say that greyhounds, whippets, salukis, borzois and deer-hounds have always, throughout the years, generally been referred to as "gaze-hounds", i.e., they hunt entirely by sight.

In Victorian times, the Waterloo Cup attracted daily crowds of 75,000 to watch greyhounds compete against the turning skill and tenacity of wild hares, but, with the arrival from America of track racing using a mechanical hare in 1926, the latter form of sport became more popular and by 1932 the total attendance at all the tracks in the UK was 20 million. This inevitably led to a decline in the numbers of those attending hare coursing meetings, although they continued to have a relatively small but very dedicated following right up until being outlawed by the 2004 Hunting Act.

In amongst it all, some whippet breeders in certain parts of the country did, between the two World Wars (and possibly beyond), indulge in the illegal practice of "rabbit racing". This involved freshly caught wild rabbits being released onto a sawdust marker some 60 yards or so in front of two competing whippets. The track was generally enclosed and, not knowing the ground, the quarry did not always run and was, in almost every case, easily caught by one or other of the dogs.

Rabbit racing was often organised by a pub landlord and held on land behind his premises – as was "rag racing" which was, unlike chasing pre-captured rabbits, completely legitimate. A rag racing track was normally open and the distance (about 200yds) paced out from start to finish on fairly level ground. Dogs would be trained for the sport right from the outset and the best breeders and trainers made sure that a duster or piece of rag was available for a litter of pups to play with just as soon as they were able. As Phil Drabble noted in his book, *Of Pedigree Unknown*, "By the time they were ten weeks old they would career about the kitchen, chasing the cloth their master waved in front of them and hang on, swinging clear of the ground, like bulldogs, when they caught it." By the time they were ready to train properly, they would then be so excited by the sight of a square of rag or towel that chasing it and tearing it became the only thing in the world that they wanted to do.

Once old enough to race, all the trainers had to do was hold them whilst the rag-men backed slowly up the length of the track, not only waving a towel, but also inciting them further by calling, shouting and whistling. When all was ready, an official starter would fire a pistol – but not before calling out "Ready, Steady, Now!" At the sound of "Ready", the handler would lift all four feet of his dog clear of the ground; at "Steady" he would swing him back an arm's length, and then, just as soon as the pistol went off, he would physically propel his dog forward, loosing it in mid-air. According to Drabble, "a good handler could 'throw' his dog five yards up the track to land him smoothly in his stride at full speed (and) it was partly this superb team-work 'twixt man and dog that gave the sport its charm."

Lure coursing in France
21st March 2012

I have, over the years I've lived in France, occasionally been asked about the opportunities for coursing here. Whilst from all I've been able to find out, hare coursing seems to be illegal; the sport of lure racing – not dissimilar in some ways to the rag racing of old – is quite popular among the owners of sight hounds.

Known as "lure-coursing", the various breed clubs hold regular meetings at which their dogs are loosed onto a bundle of rags, or strips of plastic ribbon, which have been fixed to the end of a line and is mechanically propelled around a make-shift race track on the grass of some agreeable farmer's field. Like rag racing, the track might be quite short, 200 metres or so, or, for some of the long-distance breeds, maybe up to a kilometre in length; in which case, the route might even include some sort of naturally occurring obstacle like a bank or stream. The idea is to simulate what might be encountered when pursuing a live hare or deer.

Judges position themselves at a good vantage point and competing dogs are slipped by their owners (rather than in the days of hare coursing when a man known as a "slipper" would have undertaken the task). Wearing a colour in order to easily differentiate between them, dogs are marked on a points system wherein each individual is marked for various attributes such as speed, turning ability and staying power. The one that "kills" the lure will be awarded additional, all-important points.

A group of French "sight-hounds".

Some clubs run their own versions of lure racing for fun, but in order to compete in national events, owners must be members of a local club. Their dogs must be registered with the French equivalent of the Kennel Club and been verified as conforming to breed standards by a recognised breed judge. They should also possess a certificate issued by the club as a result of an animal fulfilling all the above criteria. After all this, the Société Centrale Canine (the French Kennel Club) will issue a "log-book", in which should be noted information such as the date, results and judges' comments resulting from every competition in which the dog participates.

Opinions based on ignorance
7th September 2011
A well aimed, firm (but reasonably gentle) kick under the table warned me that, in the interest of marital harmony, I should keep quiet during a recent supper conversation whilst out with acquaintances! Knowing me as she obviously does, my wife realised that the discussion might have got a little heated when, from goodness knows where, the subject of the Waterloo Cup was raised.

Those around the table all had an opinion on the event but knew so little about the subject that they were under the impression that it was still being held annually and had no idea that it had been affected by the Hunting Act. The usual emotive language of "hares being ripped to pieces" was used and it was presented as fact that hares were caught elsewhere, transported to the venue and then released in front of the running dogs on the day.

As every countryman knows, hares need to be well acquainted with their immediate surroundings in order to give the best of themselves and, if individuals had been released fresh in front of the dogs, there would be none of those exciting twists and turns which can be seen only when an animal is fully aware of its own locality – and, without those twists and turns, there would be no way of judging the skills and merits of individual dogs.

Of course it was opined that the reason two dogs were used was to ensure the hare was caught – never once did anyone seem aware of the fact that it was often the greyhound that had done the most "work" that was awarded points rather than the one that might have actually caught and killed the hare. Nor was it considered that, percentage-wise, very few hares were actually killed.

Despite my wifely warning, I did dare venture to suggest that the holding of the Waterloo Cup was a good exercise in conservation as it meant hare stocks were monitored and that all which could possibly be done to ensure a plentiful and healthy number of hares stock was carried out. Those around the table gave me quizzical and disbelieving looks – especially when I pointed out that, generally, when no conservation, whether of hares or game birds, is carried out by those interested in coursing, hunting or shooting, it will not be long before numbers suffer due to predation and poaching.

Another thing that was most certainly not considered was the revenue that the three-day event used to bring into the area. With tens of thousands visiting annually, the Waterloo Cup was an occasion eagerly anticipated by the local hoteliers, pubs, restaurants and shopkeepers. Nor was the tradition mentioned and, having been held on the Altcar estate since 1836, and long been an annual pilgrimage for all manner of coursing enthusiasts, it would be fair to say that there was certainly plenty of that.

Coursing as a purist sport has never been just about killing hares!

Coursing as a purist sport has never been about killing hares – but try telling that to those who were sitting around the supper table when the subject of the Waterloo Cup arose the other evening!

<u>Spanish sight-hounds</u>
1st May 2013

Due to the fact that, in general terms, coursing has been illegal in France since 1844, it is quite rare to see sight-hounds of any description. There are, though, some hunting dogs which I suspect must have, in their past breeding, a touch of greyhound judging by their deep rib-cages and ambling gait when observed from behind. They are all quite tall at the shoulder, though, and I've yet to see any types that stand at only 16 to 18 inches – which are quite commonplace in the UK.

Spanish hunters have a breed of sight-hound known as the Galgo, several of which are rescued by the French after being abandoned by their owners once the shooting season has finished. Sadly, Spanish field sports enthusiasts are not generally well-known for their caring attitude towards their animals and although some are well enough treated, this is not the case for every Galgo kept by the inhabitants of rural southern Spain who happen to like a spot of hare hunting. The lucky ones end up in privately run Spanish shelters (there are apparently, no animal protection laws in Spain) and fortunately, some are befriended and adopted by new French owners who are prepared to take the time and money to bring them to a better life over the border.

Because of the old laws, they or indeed, any type of sight-hound cannot be used in France for the purpose for which they are bred – and most certainly not at night as lamping of any description is also frowned upon by the French authorities.

Dogs on film
22nd February 2012

When it comes to working dogs being portrayed in films or on television, forget the likes of Rin-Tin-Tin (a German Shepherd) or Lassie (a show-type collie) and instead think sporting dogs of the kind that are quite likely to be associated with all who have an interest in field sports. Currently being shown in the press and all manner of media is the rather good-looking terrier which has stolen the hearts of many by his fine acting and personality in the box office hit, _The Artist_. Sadly, as characterful a dog as he appears, I don't think we can count the computer-generated fox-terrier "Snowy" who appears in the latest version of Tintin which appeared on screen towards the end of last year!

Perhaps even more successful than either of those is the television programme _Downton Abbey_ and it was interesting to see included in their "Christmas Special", a shooting sequence which featured, albeit briefly, several working gundogs – all of which were actually owned and worked by keepers and others who would normally be involved in a shooting day. In general, though, getting known well enough to have film and television producers wanting to use your dogs is not easy and, if you are serious about one day having a famous dog, you will probably require the services of an agent. More often than not, however, as in the case of those on screen in *Downton Abbey*, it's more a matter of being in the right place at the right time.

Whenever a period piece is required on film or television, a dog of a breed known at the time will be required by the producers and researchers. If an example of the breed is well trained (as hopefully most keepers" and sporting dogs are), there's an opportunity to take advantage of such a situation! I once was charged with keeping a cocker spaniel of mine sitting looking quizzically despite the acting star's efforts to get it to come towards her (a firm out-stretched hand used almost universally as a "stop" signal as I was standing out of shot behind the actress in question did the trick). In addition, a friend's spaniel once appeared as Elizabeth Barrett Browning's dog Flush and another's guard dog English mastiff was chosen as Emily Brontë's dog Keeper in a dramatised television documentary about the author's life.

Packs of hounds are regularly used on both film and television and, when you think about it, it is surprising just how many times a hunting scene appears, particularly on television. Even programmes such as *Midsomer Murders* have featured hounds and hunting and of course, many of the period dramas (including *Downton Abbey*) show, or have shown, elegant ladies riding side-saddle whilst following a supposed hunt. My personal favourite of all these was the *Irish R. M.* series, based on the books of Somerville and Ross, which appeared on Channel 4 between 1983-1985.

Many sporting dogs have appeared in adverts too. Possibly the most famous of these is Jason, the basset hound who featured in the logo for Hush Puppies shoes. Less known to those of us who prefer a quiet rural life to a frenetic night life is Ulysses, the "Basset Rave Hound" who has become the mascot of various night clubs and music festivals in Britain and Europe. Ulysses has been photographed with many famous DJ's at such venues and apparently even has his own fan page on Facebook!

Possibly the earliest advert featuring a sporting dog is the one for phonographs which first appeared in 1910. "Nipper" was a terrier belonging to English painter Francis Barruad and a portrait of his dog entitled "His Master's Voice" eventually became the advertising image of the Gramophone Company and is still well-known today.

Labradors are often chosen by advertisers because of their wholesome, family-friendly personality. Although there are many examples, the one which springs most readily to people's minds is the "Andrex Puppy". Since 1972, there have been over 130 television adverts featuring Labrador puppies playing with rolls of toilet paper and the "Andrex Puppy" is the only brand icon to appear in Madame Tussauds.

Not all dog adverts have been successful and there was a huge public outcry when John Lewis at Christmas 2010 showed a dog – a rough-coated lurcher, I think (although at the time it was claimed to be a deerhound), kennelled outside in the snow.

As with their film and TV appearances, sporting dogs can sometimes become an advertising ally by accident. Dave Small, of "Reedlands Retrievers" tells of when, at a very hot and sunny county show, one of his dogs sloped away from his stand in search of somewhere even more sheltered. Discovering the relative cool of a nearby clothing suppliers tent far more to her liking, she settled under a display of sporting apparel and

Producers and actors – both human and canine – prepare for a "take" for a scene in the popular television series, Downton Abbey (courtesy of Nicola Small).

spent a happy time there until her master found her and made to take her back ... only to be met with a request from the stand holder to leave her where she was because, "she's attracted more people and so sold far more trousers and coats than I've ever managed to do."!

A last resting place
7th May 2013

Given that most country people have a dog and, bearing in mind, the oft-quoted mantra of one year of a dog's life supposedly being equivalent to seven human years, most of us are likely to mourn the death (and celebrate the life) of several during our own biblical life span of three-score years and ten. Despite the fact that our fellow field-sportsmen might not agree, we all think of our own working dogs as being perfect; not only do they give pleasure and perform a useful task out in the field, they are also often an important part of the household and there is, therefore, huge heartache when a dog becomes old or infirm and has to be put down.

An option not open to most of us but one which was in vogue with many sportsmen of the past, is a private dog graveyard – some of which can still be found in the grounds of an estate. With money no object, individual memorials might be basic or bizarre, ornate or ordinary, but the fact remains that they were erected with love for a particular canine companion. Lucinda Lambton, in her book _Palaces for Pigs_ (English Heritage, 2011), mentions the skills of Martin Cook, a fourth generation master mason who, when her "grey-brindle, rough-haired, whiskered lurcher" died at two years of age due to having run into a spear of stick whilst running after a Muntjac deer, agreed to construct an obelisk which was erected over the dog's final resting place in her garden at Hedgerley, Buckinghamshire.

Elsewhere, a working terrier named Tim is buried under a quite ornate sun-dial in a private garden in Gloucestershire, a sun-dial being chosen because, according to his owner, "he never knew when to come home". Likewise, in a garden in Hampshire stands a cast life-size image of Jason, a Labrador who was much loved despite the fact that he was not known for his obedience to the "return" whistle when sent out on a retrieve: he did, though, according to his owner, "always eventually come back with something ... whether or not it had been shot."!

Royalty is not averse to commemorating the life of a favourite canine either – as can be seen by this particular epitaph recorded as being on a gravestone at Adelaide Cottage, Windsor:

"Here lies Dash, the Favourite Spaniel of Queen Victoria
By whose command this Memorial was erected.
He died on the 20 December, 1840 in his 9th year.
His attachment was without selfishness,
His playfulness without malice,
His fidelity without deceit.
Reader, if you would live beloved and die regretted, profit by the example
of DASH"

At Sandringham, there are a series of plaques set into a wall; each of which commemorates the life of one of the present Queen's gundogs. Typical of the inscriptions is this one:

"Black Labrador
F.T.W. Sandringham Brae
24.2.82-10.5.92
A Gentleman amongst dogs"

However, bearing in mind how much we all love our dogs, perhaps most appropriate to the majority is a plaque inserted into the walled garden of an estate in North Yorkshire, on which it says; "Close to this spot lies Lucy – a Lurcher. A crossbred to others, she was perfect to us."

6

People and Places

ONE of the many joys of field sports is that, no matter how many people you know, or how many places you have previously visited, you are always going to meet more during the course of a year! Over-wintering in England because of my "meeting and greeting" job on the West Sussex estate, I have had the opportunity to both stay in contact with old gamekeeping friends and meet new acquaintances as a result of chatting with invited Guns. In France, I have become great friends with Maurice, our somewhat tongue-in-cheek sporting neighbour, and Patrice, the one-time owner of the local game farm. No matter where or when, it's impossible not to have enjoyed and learned a great deal from all of these encounters.

My parents always used to worry when I spent my early teenage years with "old men". Not, I hasten to add in the same way that parents might today, but because they felt I should be spending my time with my own peer group. I could never understand their worries because, to me, those with experience were far more interesting and could teach me a great deal about the subjects I found fascinating.

Without these "old boys" I would never have learned what I did about chicken-keeping, terriers, hunting, shooting, and 101 other country orientated topics. It is frequently said, when a respected countryman dies, that "we shall never see their like again" but hopefully, there will always be more to follow on.

PEOPLE ...

Every field sport needs continuation. Here in France, whilst youngsters undoubtedly participate by going along with their fathers in a shooting foray round the commune, those that actually shoot are, in the main, 40 years plus in age. What happens to the interim generation I've not yet managed to fathom and it's so unlike the situation in Britain where many late teenagers and 20 and 30 year olds enjoy some exciting shooting.

In Britain, hunting seems to encourage youngsters to follow hounds but, a little like the situation with shooting in France, while there may be several teenagers on horseback – and plenty of people following who are middle-aged and upwards – where are the 20 and 30 year olds? Maybe it is simply a case of financially care-free teenagers enjoying the sport whilst "sponsored" by their parents and then spending valuable time building a career and being distracted by marriage and families before they are eventually in a position to return to such things in their 40s?

As an example, whilst trail-hunting with the beagles has an undoubtedly healthy following of college-aged followers (many of which are huntsmen

Field sports are full of twinkle-eyed characters!

and whippers-in), the "field" is quite often made up of only retired people. But perhaps my observation is unfounded as, on my most recent forays onto the beagling field, it has been to the mid-week meets when it might reasonably be expected that most people will be at work. When I whipped-in to beagles in my youth, there were always pensioners in the field – from my recent observations there obviously still are – and they cannot be one and the same generation. Perhaps then, things are continuing as they always have and "characters" like our French neighbour Maurice ('The Sporting Oracle') will continue to add to the enjoyment of a day's sport!

The musings of Maurice
15th September 2010

Maurice is an enthusiastic member of "le chasse" with a great tongue-in-cheek sense of humour. His home "Le Beaumont" which lies across the vines from us, is, or so he maintains, the very nerve centre of Europe and, whilst he might be deluding himself on that front, his local knowledge is second to none. He and I have, over the years I've lived here, entered into various ill-fated enterprises such as the time we decided to try and rear and release some grey partridges. In amongst his typically French attitude and all his mickey-taking, Maurice does, however, always have something interesting to say. Quite where he gets all his information from I've no idea, perhaps "Le Beaumont" is indeed the centre of sporting Europe after all because seemingly unconnected gossip on one particular day I visited varied from local to national field sports issues.

Apparently, according to him, the local "sanglier" or wild boar population is on the increase and there has been a great deal of evidence of young boar seen around the vineyards where they have been rooting out vines freshly planted in the spring. Although I'd not observed any obvious signs on my morning walks, I have noticed that many of these immature vines have been recently protected with double strands of electric fencing. Now I know why.

Maurice has a relative employed by the "Fédération des chasseurs", the Gard department offices of which were, in the spring of this year, deliberately vandalised by an arson attack from the French Animal Liberation Front who later admitted to their guilt via an internet blog.

Despite their admission, no criminal proceedings have been forthcoming and just what Maurice had to say on the matter can be easily imagined!

Although the incident itself is not at all funny, the way Maurice told me of the plight of one of the brown bears recently re-introduced into the Pyrenees from Slovenia caused me to smile. Wild bears currently living in France number only 20 or so, but the birth of two cubs was enough to feature during the relevant stage of this year's Tour de France in July when both pro and anti bear protestors made sure their slogans were seen by the world's media. However, it was the way in which one of the adult bears, fortunately not the mother of the cubs, had died that caused the somewhat ironic amusement as, according to Maurice, it seems that it was killed by simply ambling into the path of a French military vehicle – one can just imagine the driver trying to explain the resultant damage to his army superiors!

As I say, for a man who tends to travel no further than a few kilometres from home, Maurice seems to have his finger on the pulse of what is going on in the field sports world throughout France as well as every bit of gossip from within the commune.

Sad news
16th January 2013

We had three let days at the West Sussex shoot during Christmas week but then there was a long enough gap for my wife and me to get back to France for the New Year. So, after I'd seen the last guest Guns away on the Saturday there was just time enough to gather a few things together and set off for the Portsmouth-Le Havre ferry.

I'm glad that it was the Saturday evening we were travelling rather than the Friday as Friday had been a wet and wild windy night and the overnight crossing would not have been all that pleasant – nor too would it have been on the following evening when conditions in the Channel were, apparently, even worse!

Arriving home to "Le Malineau" at lunchtime on the Sunday, we'd not done much more than unpack a few groceries and light the wood burner when two members of the local chasse who we now know quite well wandered past the house and, seeing us there, stopped and said to join them at the end of the day for a meal, a glass or two of wine and a catch-up with any news. After what had been a hectic week, I would have preferred to have stayed at home but what clinched it was the fact that they mentioned Maurice would be there.

Despite not being well enough to have been out shooting this season, Maurice nevertheless maintains contact with all of his friends involved in the commune shoot and so it was that, when I sat and talked to him later in the day, he was straight away able to tell me that René, another local farmer and one-time member of the chasse, had died … and that Bernard had been caught drink/driving and there was a chance he might lose his gun licence as a result.

It was sad news about René, but, given his health and age, not totally unexpected – he was, however, similar to Maurice in his sense of humour and in being a great raconteur so it will take a while to get used to him not being around. And, from a purely practical and mercenary point of view, it also means that we now need to find another firewood supplier!

As to the misfortunes of Bernard, that did seem a little unfair as he is not a great drinker and seemingly simply fell foul of the very strict drink/driving

"Avec moderation" (as the French say!), the odd mid-morning drink is part of a day's sport.

laws in France where, despite what one might suppose in a nation of wine-drinkers, there is actually far less tolerance than in the UK.

A lesson in tickling
20th May 2009

The first trout I ever saw caught was done so illegally by my maternal grandfather. I was only seven at the time and yet I remember it as well as anything I did yesterday. In the intervening years I've since realised that, bearing in mind where we were fishing, the demand for silence was issued just as much in order to avoid being noticed by the water bailiffs as it was for the stealth required in capturing a fish by somewhat unorthodox means. In addition, Granddad had previously instilled into me the need to approach the water's edge with stealth and to take advantage of any bank-side cover that would help in preventing casting a shadow across the water.

"See that fish," said Granddad, pointing to a dark place under some exposed roots. "Yes," I lied, not having a clue where he was looking. All of a sudden, I saw the tail of a trout, fanning idly in the current, all it needed to maintain its equilibrium in the gentle current. Typical that it was on the opposite bank and that the need to cross over was, therefore, like Armstrong's step on the moon in 1969, "one small step for man, one giant leap for Mankind". Granddad, aged 83, nipped across with great alacrity. I crossed with my leg in the ditch and scared the fish.

Patience indeed being a virtue, Granddad knew that, if we waited long enough, the fish we were after would return to its "swim" and, after five minutes or so, it did. With long, leisurely and very gentle flicks of its tail. Slowly uncoiling and shaping a piece of twisted brass wire from his pocket and attaching it to a short, thin wand of hazel twig which he'd quietly snapped from a nearby bush after ensuring that I'd made the crossing safely, my mentor gently placed the resultant noose in the water.

Inch by inch, the slow, tortuous and gentle feeding of the wire noose over the fish's body began. Just as I was thinking that we were going to miss the fish of my lifetime, Granddad brought the noose rapidly forward, caught the trout by its gills – which were naturally outstretched as it sifted air, food and plantain through its body – and hoicked it swiftly and cleanly onto the bank. Cool, calm and collected, Granddad

There was similar celebration the day we tickled a trout!.

allowed himself a gentle smile. Full of excitement, and forgetful of the fact that we were not supposed to be there, I screamed and whooped and, in that moment, the difference of 76 years between pensioner and child mattered not one jot.

A "White Christmas" in August
12th August 2005

Looking back at my diaries, 1975 seemed to have been quite an eventful season for me! Not only did I build a moorland road single-handedly and we had the excitement of the moor catching alight, but the estate also had a week-long visit from a group of Texans, one of whom had brought with him as a guest, the famous singer and crooner Bing Crosby.

About halfway through his stay, Bing asked the head keeper what we all did at the end of the shooting day and, after having it explained to him that, once we had sorted out the dead grouse for the game dealer and prepared all that needed to be done for the following day's shooting, we would most likely go to the pub; he asked if he could join us there.

So it was that, in a quiet pub in the middle of the Yorkshire moors at the end of August, we taught Bing Crosby to sing *On Ikley Moor* and he stood at the bar and crooned *White Christmas* to an enthusiastic audience of half a dozen keepers and a couple of bemused hill-farmers.

It must have been a good night because when I woke up and went outdoors the next morning, I discovered that I'd driven my van over the flower-bed and garden of where I was lodging. It was quite a while before my landlady really forgave me and even now some 40 years later, she generally manages to make reference to it in her annual Christmas card!

... AND PLACES

I've never even tried to work out the amount of British counties in which I've been fortunate enough to shoot, fish, go beating or follow hounds. Some places I can remember clearly but others were memorable either for the sport or the company I was in rather than for their location. However, even though I might not be able to clearly recall the place-names, my memory-bank thankfully still quite clearly retains the beauty or unusualness of the topography.

Apart from France, the opportunity for sport abroad has not been quite so numerous and so the people and places tend to remain more clearly fixed. One particular jaunt that will hopefully live in my mind forever was to Slovenia where, in the mountain ranges situated between Nova Gorica and Tolmin and in the central southern part of the country are the peaks of Sneznk some 1,500 metres high. In both there is breath-taking scenery and, inhospitable though some of the landscape may appear, wildlife and game can be found in abundance. Sitting in the sunshine on the patio of Branko Gašparin, a fishing guide, shooting enthusiast and taxidermist of note, whilst overlooking the valleys and still snow-topped mountains with a glass of wine from his own vineyard in hand, I clearly remember thinking "can life get any better than this?"

A Slovenian sojourn
19th May 2010

Volcanic ash very nearly put paid to my recent trip to Slovenia as it was just 24 hours before we were due to leave that the flying restrictions were lifted. Had I not have been able to travel I would have missed out on a wonderful week or so finding out about field sports in this most beautiful of east European countries. Slovenia might be small but everyone seems very friendly and the lifestyle just as laid back as France – no wonder I felt immediately at home there!

Coarse fishing doesn't have quite the same appeal in Slovenia as does fly-fishing which has such a reputation that people from all over the world visit in order to try and catch the unique Marble trout (salma trutta marmoratus) to be found in the river Zadlaščia which flows through the Triglav National Park near the town of Tolmin. The Marble trout is, according to our fishing guide Branko Gašparin, a beast that can grow up to 140cm in length and weigh up to 24kg. Its existence was at one time, seriously threatened by the introduction of brown trout as up until then, any naturally occurring "brownies" had been prevented from entering the places where the Marble trout lived and bred by the barriers of rock pools and cascading waterfalls. As a result, brown trout are not nowadays stocked in the most sensitive rivers, but there is plenty of potential to catch them – along with rainbow and grayling – in the rivers Soča, Uča, Bača and Vipava. Some local knowledge is, however, imperative: a guide is likely to be able to tell you the relevant water and weather conditions and, as a result, suggest areas where successful fishing is most likely.

As in France, shooting and stalking is known in Slovenia by the generic term "hunting". There is hunting available on both private and state-owned land, all of which is extremely well managed in respect of sporting activities. As far as game bird shooting in particular is concerned, it is not permitted to shoot snipe or woodcock, but there are plenty of opportunities to be had with pheasant, grey partridge – there are no red-legs – mallard, quail and hares. Depending on where you are, it is either walked up over dogs, or driven as in the UK. Seasons vary between north and south, east and west, but generally begin around September 1st for mallard, partridge and pheasant.

Pheasants have been found in Slovenia since the end of the 19th Century where they were introduced for the sporting benefit of counts and other landed gentry. Wild bird numbers subsequently grew until the 1970s when they suffered a complete contrast of fortune because of a change in agricultural activities. In the north-east of the country I visited the state hunting area around Beltinci where we were shown around by the head of hunting for the region. Dragan Zemljič is, together with 13 wardens or gamekeepers, responsible for over 15,000 hectares onto which are released 35,000 pheasant and 5,000 grey partridge, all of which helps to augment the wild stock.

Woodland management in this area is carried out as an incidental "by-product" of farmers cutting wood for fuel; this helps regeneration and the hedgerows and small coppices certainly appear to be thriving under such methods. The farmers are not so helpful in other ways though and there are problems with wild bird stocks as a result of the use of herbicides and the cutting of silage at a time when hen birds are nesting. Food is supplied on a year round basis by the use of hoppers similar to those used in the UK.

Due to government legislation, predator control can be a bit of a problem and there are bans preventing the killing of foxes during their breeding season: a time when one would most need to in order to protect breeding game birds. It is however, permissible to use terriers for fox control. Crow numbers can only be reduced by shotguns and, judging by Dragan's blank expression when we asked him, there would appear to be no use of Larson traps or cage traps.

Interestingly, it is also forbidden to shoot pigeons at any time of year. This strange fact was apparently brought about in an effort to appease the "green" anti-hunting lobby; the reasoning being, as Dragan described it, "the shooters thought if we give them our hand, they will not eat our arm!" Likewise, and probably for the same reason, goose shooting of any kind is not permitted.

Guns mostly come from Slovenia, Austria and Italy – the Italians apparently being very keen on hare shooting, a privilege for which they are happy to pay 80 euros per hare. Unlike the UK where you might buy a day's shooting and pay in advance on the basis of an anticipated bag, in Slovenia, you only pay for the game laid out on the ground at the end of the day. Typically, it will cost 16 euros per pheasant, 18 euros a partridge and 13 euros per mallard. On top of this, there is a tax of 33 euros charged

In Slovenia, the river Zadlaščia flows through the Triglav National Park – and is the home of the unique Marble trout: difficult fishing but, from experience, well worth the effort!

to each hunter. On state hunting grounds, which have been in existence since 1950, it is not necessary to have a licence – association or "family" shooting is different – and, according to Dragan Zemljič, bag numbers can vary between 50 and 400 depending on how big a day one might prefer (or can afford!). Dragan is also very keen on falconry and it is possible to have a day out with him after pheasant or partridge. I have already booked to do just that in the not-too-distant future!

Down at the old Bull and Bush
18th August 2010

Hotels, inns and public houses have always been associated with field sports. Hounds have met in front of them for years; shooting parties and fishermen stay and dine there and various affiliated clubs find them a useful venue at which to convene meetings. Their names also often have a link to field sports; the "Fox and Hounds" is perhaps the most obvious, but there are others such as "The Gamekeeper", or "Keeper's Arms" and "The Compleat Angler", named of course after Sir Isaak Walton's famous book of the same name.

Much of Walton's book deals with fishing in Buckinghamshire – and there is a well-known hotel of the same name at Marlow – but "The Trout" at Lower Wolvercote, near Oxford has been equally as famously portrayed in Colin Dexter's *Inspector Morse* stories as well as by writers such as C. S. Lewis and Lewis Carroll, the latter of course, being famous for writing *Alice in Wonderland*.

Some establishments which, from their name, you might justifiably think have a fishing connection have not: there was, for instance, a pub in South Shields that was known as the "Balancing Eel" which actually came by its name as a result of a verse in Lewis Carroll's *Alice in Wonderland*: "You are old said the youth one would hardly suppose/That your eye was as steady as ever;/Yet you balanced an eel on the end of your nose –/what made you so awfully clever?" Sadly, the place is now apparently known by the far less interesting name of the "Bizz Bar".

As well as the obvious "Fox and Hounds", there are also several pubs named the "Hare and Hounds" and, at Brendon, Somerset, can be found the "Stag Hunters". Still on the stag hunting theme, the "Stag Hunt" in the village of Ponsanooth in Cornwall supposedly gets its name from Roman times, but in actual fact whether the Romans hunted deer during their occupation of the British Isles is a mute point. At Swimbridge, North Devon is located the "Jack Russell" pub, the sign for which, the last time I was there in the early 1990s, depicted a portrait of Russell's original terrier Trump, but I believe before that, it showed a portrait of the parson himself. At Bowness on Windermere in the Lake District, John Peel, another famous huntsman is remembered in the name of the local inn, which also houses what are purported to be Peel's hunting crop and stirrups.

Some pubs have no obvious reference to hunting in their name, but have, nevertheless, close associations with the sport. Under the window of the "Sun Inn" at Bilsdale, North Yorkshire, for instance, is a tombstone intended for Bobbie Dawson who was, for 60 years, whipper-in to the

Bilsdale Hunt. When he died at the beginning of the last century at the ripe old age of 86, local folk subscribed for a stone to be erected over his grave. The parson, however, objected as the carving on the stone depicted a fox's mask, brush and whip. So a plain stone was erected over the grave and the locals installed the original memorial outside the pub from which the old man had often set out on a day's hunting. Apparently, at his funeral, Bobbie's favourite brown hunter, his spurs, cap and the Bilsdale hunting horn followed the cortege but it is not recorded what the vicar thought of that!

At Woodlands in the New Forest is the "Gamekeeper" pub and its sign is interesting in the fact that, when a new one was commissioned in 2008, the publican Mark Thompson asked the artist to include his cocker spaniel Charlie as one of the three dogs depicted in the painting. Other sporting dogs to appear in pub signs are those appertaining to any establishments known as the "Dog and Partridge", most of which feature either a pointer or setter. It is said that the first Labrador dog ever brought into Britain was owned by a Weymouth licensee, and that it was he who named his inn the "Black Dog" – the first of many such pub names.

There are also plenty of "Dog and Duck" public houses and, in connection with hawking, many drinking and eating establishments known as the "Falcon". There are various theories about the name "Hawk & Buckle" which is found in several parts of the country. The most likely is that the word buckle is a corruption of the French "boucle" meaning buckle or swivel. "En boucle" in French can also mean imprisoned and, as a hawk when not flying is often tethered to a perch or block by means of a leash at the end of which is a swivel, it seems quite likely that an imprisoned or tethered hawk would be termed a "hawk en buckle"; which in time, could have been further anglicised to create the pub's moniker. Another drinking house with a strange name was the "Wig and Fidgett" at Boxted, Colchester, Essex. It is sadly no longer trading but by far the most plausible explanation for its name is that the words stemmed from old English wig deriving from whicken, meaning white, and fitchet, being an old name for a polecat.

Some sporting links remain in pub names long after what they originally commemorated was made illegal. Cock-fighting was banned in 1847 but there are still several references in names such as the "Gamecock" and the "Cock". In the "Cockpit Tavern", London, customers at the bar stand on what was originally the cock-pit floor. The famous "Bear" hotel at Woodstock is not, however, as one might suppose, the past venue for bear-baiting, but was, quite bizarrely, used for bull-baiting – as was the more obviously named "Bull Ring" in Ludlow, Shropshire.

Many of today's pub signs are works of art, but in times gone by they were simply a way of the mainly illiterate general public identifying a particular building. In 1393, Richard II decreed that all public houses must have a sign in order that ale-testers would know the location of each property. Ale-testers…nice work if you can get it!

The "Fox and Hounds" is probably the most common of pub signs associated with field sports.

Fit for a king
29th June 2011

Chambord is just one of the many châteaux to be found along the Loire Valley: it is undoubtedly the largest, but though magnificent, perhaps not the prettiest as that honour supposedly goes to the Château d'Ussé on the edge of the Chinon forest. In fact, tradition has it that when Charles Perrault, the famous French writer of fairy tales, was looking for a setting for Sleeping Beauty, he chose Ussé as his model. Fairy-tale looks though it might have, Ussé, unlike Chambord, cannot claim to have been the venue for the French Game Fair for the past 30 years, nor was it built mainly as a hunting lodge.

As a young man, François I liked to hunt in the nearby forest of Boulogne and in 1518 he ordered the old castle to be razed in order to make room for a construction more like a palace than a hunting lodge. Several architects put ideas forward (including, it is believed, Leonardo da Vinci) and the building changed in design as François continuously adapted the original plans. There's no doubt as to what this particular king's priorities were: despite his government coffers being empty and the fact that he was reduced to raiding the treasuries of the churches or to melting down his subjects' silver, he still insisted that work went on at Chambord. In his enthusiasm for the project, François even proposed to divert the course of the river Loire so that it should flow in front of the château but in view of the enormity of this task, a smaller river, the Cosson, was chosen instead.

Once the work was eventually completed, François II, Charles IX and Louis XIV were amongst the well-known royals who came frequently to hunt in the surrounding forests. It is said that Louis XII would take 16ft (5m) ditches on horseback without flinching and that, despite his well-known delicate constitution, Charles IV would hunt for as long as 10 hours at a time, exhausting at least five horses and often coughing up blood in the process. Records have it that he also once hunted down a stag without the aid of hounds but sadly, fail to recount how he managed this particular triumph!

During the peak of its sporting life, Chambord was well stocked with game and there was a great deal of hawking (the Royal Mews once boasted over 300 falcons) and hunting. The resident pack of hounds were extremely well looked after and unrelated bloodlines from other

Chambord – a little more "up-market" than the average hunting lodge!

hunting establishments were brought in from all over Europe in order to continually update and improve the Royal strain. The various kings hunting at Chambord used to give their particular huntsman a nickname and this custom still persists today with many professional huntsmen throughout France adopting traditional titles such as "Daguet", "La Futaie" and "Sauteaubois".

Since 1948, the park surrounding Chambord has been a national reserve for "le chasse" and covers some 13,600 acres. No wonder then, that, what with both modern and ancient sporting connections, the château was chosen, way back in 1981, to be the permanent venue for the annual French Game Fair.

"Vive la Revolution"
13th July 2011

Tomorrow (14 July) is Bastille Day here in France, although amongst the French people themselves, it is almost universally known as "Quatorze Juillet". Whatever, it is yet another bank holiday and almost every village and town has its own way of celebrating. Almost all do, however, culminate with a fireworks display of one form or another so there will be little if any chance of the nation's dog population escaping the unsettling bangs and flashes.

The day originated in commemoration of the French Revolution which began with the storming of the Bastille prison in 1789. Before this time, France was officially and legally divided into three orders: the clergy, the nobility ... and everyone else, known simply as "the third estate". Throughout the 18th Century, the number of wealthy people amongst the latter group grew in size and began to outstrip the nobility in monetary terms, buying land and property as if it was going out of fashion. Nevertheless, despite their new affluence, they remained inferior in status. You could be the richest man in the country, but if you didn't have the ear of the King and his court, you couldn't even get a fishing licence, let alone permission to hunt or hawk. So, when the Bastille was stormed on 14 July that year, there were as many, if not more, of the land-owning faction as there were "peasants" and "commoners" amongst the crowds.

As far as field sports were concerned, the Revolution and subsequent dispersal of the French aristocracy turned out to have the opposite effect to that which was hoped for and actually brought about a curtailment of most elements of "le chasse", in particular, hunting with hounds. Whilst it continued in limited form throughout the following century and a half, it was not until the end of the Second World War that the majority of packs nowadays seen in France came into existence.

Certain canine bloodlines were, however, kept alive by farmers and shepherds maintaining small packs of rough-coated hounds in order to keep control of wild boar and wolves in densely-wooded areas such as the Morvan. Evidence of this can be found in an account of the early 1800s where a certain M. Brière d'Azy was being troubled by wolves and he wrote to a relation in the Vendée requesting some hounds: he received the following curt and somewhat laconic reply: "I am sending thirteen hounds with a huntsman called Charrier, the animals are perfect, the man better."

As far as shooting was concerned, wild game stocks were eventually enhanced (despite phenomenal poaching) as a result of Napoleon's post-Revolution laws, many of which put landownership in the hands of the ordinary people. Inheritance laws that still exist today insisted that, when a farmer died, his land had to be split equally between his children. When they subsequently passed on, their land was divided between their offspring and so on – which is why so many individuals now own so many small plots of land throughout France.

A grand day out
15th August 2009

August 15th is yet another bank holiday in France – and is always the date of the annual "fête de la chasse" held at the Parc du Lathon just north of Saumur in the Loire Valley. Although there are many similar throughout France, this particular fête de la chasse is one of the best of its kind and is temporary home on the day to many packs of hounds and terriers, as well as being the permanent location for the kennels of M. Olivier de La Bouillerie and his private pack, the "Rallye des Grands Loups".

Apart from just one or two alterations in the mid-afternoon programme, nothing much changes from year to year, but the event is no less interesting for that. The day starts around 9.00am (remember it's France and time is not so important here!) and hound and terrier judging is the first thing on the agenda. Hounds are paraded in front of the judges in groups of six,

M. Olivier de La Bouillerie and his private pack, the "Rallye des Grands Loups".

after which, at around 11.00am, there is the Mass of St Hubert, the patron saint of hunting.

Throughout the day there is a "concours de trompe" or horn-blowing competition where the huge curled French hunting horns are blown to quite melodious effect. Visiting packs of hounds and terriers are kept in the shade of the trees and can be visited at any time they are not being shown or paraded. There's working tests for pointing and setting dogs, archery, and various interesting trade stands selling sporting art, guns, taxidermy, saddles and bridles, shooting clothing and knives – pretty much everything you'd usually find at any such event.

It being France, lunch takes priority and there's usually a two-hour break between noon and two o'clock in order to allow for this most sacred of rituals. Then, on the lawns of the chateau begin the parade of hounds at which anywhere between 40-50 packs of hare, fox, wild boar and deer hunting hounds are shown to the public. Spectators stand on the bank of the canal which divides the main show area from the chateau grounds and, sometimes, but not always, are treated to the spectacle of a mounted M. de La Bouillerie dressed in full hunting gear and accompanied by his hounds, launching themselves into the canal and swimming part of its length – a leap of trust and faith on the part of horse and hounds, I think!

In the evening, there are several displays – which might be as diverse as traditional singing, a falconry demonstration, or a drag hunt performed by one of the visiting packs. As is usual on such occasions, prize-giving and presentations are made to the hound show winners and successful contestants of the horn-blowing competition. And then, as dusk falls, the day finishes with a quite spectacular firework display.

7

A Wealth of Wildlife

O
UT in the countryside, whether it is in Britain or France, there's always something new to learn from observing wildlife – either whilst out walking or when enjoying a day's sport. A conversation with a certain Philippe Ferrero was very interesting, not least because of the fact that buzzards are generally accepted to be mainly carrion eaters. Very roughly translated, Philippe's recollections went something like this; "On a cold morning at the end of December, I was looking for woodcock with my dog, Story. Suddenly, the dog raised a woodcock. To my surprise, I saw a bird – without doubt a buzzard, appear and make off with the woodcock. In my surprise and to scare off the bird, I let out a cry and the buzzard let go of the woodcock, which fell about 80m to the ground. My dog and I went to search for the little bird. Story went on point and I recovered the woodcock, which had been injured, but not killed by the hawk."

Wild boar are omnivores
11th April 2007

Conservationists and field sportsmen – they should be one and the same thing, but whilst I could agree that most, if not all, field sportsmen are conservationists, I cannot unfortunately say that the same criteria applies the other way around – seem to be disagreeing about the contents of a wild boar's stomach.

Heinz Meynhart, a German-born naturalist now living in France, has recently investigated the stomach contents of several "sanglier" and decided that they are not as entirely vegetarian as was once supposed. According to his findings, only 90 percent of the wild boar's diet is vegetable in origin, the other 10 percent consisting of insects, bird's eggs, plus a surprising amount of fresh water mussels, snails and amphibians – all found around the edges of many ecologically important areas of marshland.

Other naturalists have also "proven" what real countrymen such as Maurice, our shooting neighbour, have known for ages and have now decided that its carnivorous habits are contributing to the decline of all small game and reptiles – with the result that whereas before, the sanglier population was only considered to be a nuisance to foresters and agriculturalists, it is now a dire threat to the entire French countryside. OK, maybe I exaggerate a little, but you know how extreme and one-sided some of these people can be!

Daniel Maillard, a representative of l'ONCFS, the organization responsible for shooting and wildlife and therefore, I suppose, the group most akin to the UKs BASC, has recently refuted their findings, saying: "All the rumours circulating apropos the impact of wild boar on small game are absurd and unfounded. They are based on suppositions and not on the basis of any serious study. I have analyzed the stomachs of over 400 boar and never discovered as much as a beak or a little feather of partridge or pheasant. On occasion, an animal will eat a bird killed or injured by the chasse and will take small rodents: they are excellent opportunists."

As with all these matters, whether they are at home or abroad, it is all a question of retaining a sense of perspective. Yes, I'm sure that wild boar will take some of the types of reptiles judged to be fragile and vulnerable, but so do adders, of which there are plenty here in France. Crows will take the young and eggs of game birds and birds of prey the adults: is there any sense in claiming that sanglier are a far more dangerous threat?

Give the lop-sided scientists and politicians who listen to them, their way and the countryside will indeed be a strange place in a very short space of time.

Wild boar are omnivores and will eat all manner of things – they do, however, quite like the easy pickings offered by an automated feeder; especially when situated over a favourite wallowing hole.

<u>What's wrong with the boar of the Ardèche?</u>
6th November 2013

About a month ago, ten wild boar were found dead within the space of seven days in the Ardèche department of France. Quite what caused their deaths seems to be something of a mystery and they were, in fact, only ten of a total of 90 that had died in similar circumstances since July of this year.

According to newspaper reports, the majority of the dead boar have been mainly found in two places: Vals-les-Bains and the valley of Eyrieux. It was first thought that they might have succumbed to a type of swine fever, or even some sort of viral disease, but laboratory analysis has since discounted these possibilities. Toxins such as pesticides or rat poison were also eliminated but, whatever the reason, in early September, it was quite sensibly decided that a prohibition on the butchering and preparing boar for human consumption should be enacted in areas surrounding 29 municipalities in the region. One thing which all seem to have had in common is that, not long before death, they appear to have suffered from nervous disorder, tremors, convulsions, spasms and "paddling" with their feet once unable to stand. As to whether whatever it is wrong with the wild boar of the Ardèche affects the local stock randomly, those currently attempting to work out the cause of the mystery deaths have noticed that it is the ones weighing between 15 and 25kg which are the most likely to succumb.

Reading this latest news reminded me of a similar situation which occurred elsewhere in France in 2011. During July and August of that year, 36 wild boar were found dead around the beaches of Normandy. Their deaths were at first thought to have been caused because of foraging on algae and seaweed which might have given off hydrogen sulphide gas as a result of nitrogen-rich waste in the sea mixing with the algae and then drying in the sun. However, autopsies and tests done on some of the wild boar carcasses subsequently found wide-ranging traces of the gas and so, as a spokesman for the local prefecture said at the time, "with such a wide difference in the values, we cannot reach any conclusion." In that particular instance, the situation got no worse and, as far as I am aware, there were no more wild boar casualties. Let's hope that the cause of whatever is currently ailing the boar population of Ardèche also burns itself out before too long.

Apart from these incidents, elsewhere in France, the population of wild boar seems incredibly healthy and their numbers are growing. Current estimates are that there around 2 million – and that fact is not popular with everybody, not least farmers and motorists. According to insurance company statistics, wild boars are responsible for over 60% of the approximately 40,000 car accidents involving wild animals annually.

As far as trouble for the farmers is concerned, it seems that they (the farmers) might be their own worst enemy and it is the increase in maize and cereal growing which has helped the boar population by providing a ready and easily available source of feed. In some places, boar are now being fed at strategic points, not just for the benefit of the revenue brought in by hunters from France and abroad, but also in an attempt to keep them away from valuable crops. However, environmentalists reckon that this might actually be worsening the problem of over-population because artificial feeding of this nature helps provide well-nourished adults and larger litters of piglets – nearly all of which reach maturity. Not only do they reach maturity, they reach it more quickly and so, it's thought, begin breeding earlier.

Recently it's been noted in the newspapers that various chasseur clubs throughout France have had to recompense farmers for wild boar damage. The farmers' argument is that the chasseurs have not done enough to control boar numbers and so, in 2011 (the latest available figures), compensation to the tune of 50 million euros was awarded and handed over. It's a fact that the viticulturalists around us are very definitely not keen on having "sounders" (herds) of wild boar about the place as they can do a great deal of damage to their vines, especially when, as this year, the grapes are late in being harvested and the boar seem to take great delight in eating them. Presumably, like the rest of us, they enjoy them because of their sweetness.

Some try and protect their vines with strands of electric fencing but then that means the grass underneath the wire has to be kept short or sprayed with weedkiller as if a fence was to short out, it wouldn't be very long before the wild boar stocks realised this and made the most of an unexpected bonus (having said that, being intelligent animals, once they

Too many wild boar in one particular area can cause untold damage to the vines and surrounding countryside.

have learned that an electric fence will give them a shock, they might be like domestic pigs and steer clear of such barriers in the future).

In the main, though, the local farmers and viticulturalists tend to try and keep boar numbers to a reasonable level by organising a few drives for them in the spring. A small pack of hounds and some strategically placed Guns seem to do the trick and the amount of boar I see on a regular basis have remained pretty constant in the decade or so we've been living here.

Personally, I like to see them around and a glimpse whilst out walking the dog first thing in the morning is an exciting sight. Perhaps the strangest thing was when, a few months back, Fideline chased a hare into a wood and then came out on the opposite side in pursuit of a wild boar! Thankfully, the boar had decided that flight was better than fight as, otherwise, the dog might have had a bit of a shock if it had decided to turn and face her!

April Fool?
4th April 2007

I am mystified. Over the last few days I've noticed a run through the hedge at the end of our track to the house becoming more and more pronounced. It's not a big hole, so it certainly is not an avenue used by roe deer and anyway, there are no slot marks.

Carefully inspecting the branches and brambles that make up the hedge itself, I cannot find any trace of hair strands left by either badger or fox and, despite its close proximity to a water-filled ditch, it is definitely not the work of coypu, because the track hasn't got that greasy look about it that so typifies their presence. I've also discounted a feral cat.

Perhaps the most mystifying aspect is the fact that, far from any "bareness" to the run, which is usually present with any regularly-used animal run, there is, every morning a fresh covering of finely-chopped vegetation. The other evening I thought I'd be clever and sweep off some of this covering with a stick so that I wouldn't leave any scent – in the hope that I'd be able to see some foot-prints or claw-marks in the morning.

Rushing up there at first light the next day, I was disappointed to see that the run had been covered over again and I'm still no closer to solving the mystery. I'm tending towards thinking it is the regular route of a hare, but if it was, there would be an obvious track leading up to it through the vineyard on the other side and there isn't.

Of course, knowing the teasing nature of our neighbour Maurice, it could be a practical joke he is playing on me – it is, after all, the week of April Fool's Day; bizarrely known here as Poisson d'Avril, or "April Fish".

Short of setting up a snare (a bit drastic) or close-circuit television (a bit expensive), it seems as if my only chance of getting the answer would be to catch a glimpse of whatever (or whoever!) it is in the car headlights as we return home from a night out.

A safe route over the motorway
16th March 2006

Compared to the M25 and any other British motorway, the French road system is a delight. There's no traffic to speak of, the road surfaces are good and a motorway journey that would take five hours in the UK, over here can be completed in three and a half. The only downside are the tolls, not just because of the cost, but also because you are monitored by the time it takes from when you take your ticket until the time you pay to exit – too fast a journey and you can be booked for speeding … or at least given a warning. Actually, there is another downside and that's the tedium associated with any long distance journey; however, the next time that you are on a mind-numbingly boring motorway in France, try looking at the bridges as a mental diversion.

There's nothing unusual about the average bridge, like most, it allows for flyovers, lets minor roads cross and gives a safe route for farmers to take tractors or livestock from one part of the farm to another. The ones of real interest to the countryman are not those with a wire support to prevent accidents, but those barricaded with timber and whose sides are slightly higher than the rest. For a nation of people that are only supposed to be happy when they are shooting something, it might be a surprise to learn that these motorway crossings are not for humans and machines, but purely for wildlife.

Because there is such a high population of large game, especially deer and wild boar throughout most of France, the land edging all motorways is sectioned off by some serious deer-type fencing. To allow free access from one side to the other, the French authorities literally build bridges to ensure that the resident wildlife population is not unnecessarily affected by Man's desire to get from A to B in the shortest possible time.

It is not an after-thought on the part of the planners either, more an integral part of the motorway network and each "wildlife" bridge is designed to funnel both small and large game safely from one side to the next without them ever being aware it being artificially made. Research in each individual area has assessed the local population of wildlife and the distances between bridges decided accordingly.

Looking up as you travel, the only indication that it is actually a "wildlife corridor" comes from the fact that the bridge has wooden sides. Were you able to stop and investigate further, you would find that the "shoulders" funnelling animals across are set at a certain angle and that the bridge has been grassed over rather than being left concrete. In addition, at each end, other grasses are planted which offer a protective cover for hares and a seasonal potential nesting site for pheasants and partridge. An oblique hedge is planted immediately behind the motorway fencing so that noise is deadened and any passing wildlife is unable to see motorway movement. In the gap between the fence and any natural woodland, normally a distance of about six metres, half-standard trees are spasmodically planted. At the immediate centre of the bridge (the narrowest point), is laid out a two metre strip of sand which is regularly checked for wildlife footprints by the local "garde particular" (a departmental gamekeeper) and the information gained is used to monitor the frequency of animal movement.

Snakes alive – or dead?
8th July 2009

The French don't like snakes – a fact I just had verified yet again when, driving home a short while ago, the car in front swerved from one side of the road in order to run over a perfectly harmless (but very large) grass snake that was weaving itself towards the cool edge of a roadside pond on the opposite verge.

Philippe, who, along with his brother grazes cattle in the fields between "Le Malineau" and our nearest neighbours, tells me that he doesn't like them for the bites the adders give his cows when the cow's slow grazing method suddenly disturb a recumbent snake – causing it to strike out. The poison does not apparently cause much damage to a full-grown beast, but does, however, result in some unpleasant hard lumps wherever it bites. Of course, young calves, with their smaller body mass may not get off as lightly.

Along with the various lizards, snakes live quite happily in the sunny spots of our garden and we have all learned to avoid the likely areas or, if we cannot, at least cause a lot of vibration by either stamping the ground with our feet, or bashing it with whatever we happen to be carrying with us at the time. There is a belief in rural France that the vibrations caused by chickens going about their daily business will keep a place clear of snakes but having frequently observed one resting in the exposed area of our own chicken run, I'm afraid that I have to discount that particular old wives' tale.

There is no reason why the French should be any more alarmed about snakes than anyone in Britain. Despite their general and irrational fear, there are no more adder bites affecting humans here than there are anywhere else – in fact, our local hospital at Thoaurs has just announced this year that it will not be keeping any anti-venom in stock because it reaches its "use-by" date long before it may possibly be required. That's not to say that an adder bite is not serious and anyone who is unfortunate enough to be bitten during the next few weeks of summer should, of course, get themselves checked out by the nearest pharmacist, doctor or at the hospital.

Despite what the rural French may think, chickens are not all that successful in frightening away snakes!

At this time of year, it makes sense to take any precaution one can to avoid dogs being bitten by adders. It is the resting snake suddenly disturbed by an over exuberant dog before it has a chance to slither off into the undergrowth that is most likely to attack. The severity of signs seen in animals as a result of snake bites is variable and depends upon several factors: these include the site of the bite and the size of the animal. Most adder bites result in pain and inflammation, but are not usually fatal. However, if your pet is bitten by an adder it should be considered to be an emergency and prompt veterinary attention should be sought, since in severe cases dogs may sometimes collapse and die following a snake bite.

An insidious menace
1st June 2011

It seems that American mink are posing a bit of a problem in Scotland, as a result of which there is government funding available for a three-year concentrated effort to control or, better still, totally eradicate their numbers. Apparently four full-time mink-catchers are to be employed specifically on the job and they will work alongside gamekeepers, farmers and landowners.

According to Scottish National Heritage, American mink can be found almost everywhere in Scotland, including the Western Isles of Harris and Lewis, and also some Hebridean islands where they have caused widespread, whole-colony breeding failures and declines in the numbers of sea birds due to their predation on eggs and chicks. Any efforts to get rid of this insidious menace has to be a good thing as they have done untold damage to native wild stocks of birds and animals throughout the whole of Britain since escaping or being deliberately released from mink farms 30 years or so ago.

Here in France, American mink numbers also need constant control. There are still some active mink farms and it was only a couple of years ago that a reported 3,000 animals were "liberated", allegedly by animal rights campaigners, from an establishment near Domme, in the Dordogne region. Whilst the trapping and shooting of feral mink is carried out whenever and wherever possible, the situation is, however, made a little more complicated in a few departments of France (including the Dordogne) due to the presence of the European mink which is classified as being endangered and is most definitely protected by law. As it is easy to confuse the two types, there is no wonder that there is a certain reticence on the part of local "gardes de chasse" and other interested parties who are, quite naturally, concerned that they might be heavily fined, or even imprisoned, should they make a mistake.

Although some extremely radical French animal rights campaigners might think it a good idea to let American mink into the countryside, there are, however, organisations such as l'ASPAS (Association pour la Protection des Animaux Sauvages) who act quite responsibly and instead of encouraging their members to break the law by releasing alien creatures into a rural environment, offer valid advice.

Through them, I have recently learned that the keeping and transport of wild animals, whether they are game animals or protected, living or dead, is forbidden in France without relevant authority from the "prefecture". Presumably, a French game licence will prevent anyone taking home the spoils of a Sunday morning's foray from being in breach of the law, and a permit to run a game farm will allow the legal transportation of pheasants and partridges from place to place, but in most other circumstances it seems that quite severe restrictions apply.

If, for instance, one happened to come across a sick or injured wild animal, you should apparently, contact the police or the local Office National de la Chasse et de la Faune Sauvage (with the long length of most organisational titles, no wonder most are simply referred to by their initials!) rather than wander off down to the vet who, in all likelihood, would be very reluctant to do anything. If he or she does agree to treat the animal or bird, it being a wild creature, they cannot charge for their services. However, that is not the reason for their reluctance and it is more to do with a fear of contravening any legalities.

Urban falconers
11th April 2007

It is, and has been for many years, common practice to use hawks as a very effective means of clearing runways just before planes are due to take off, but here in France, whilst they are regularly flown at military airports, they are also used to great effect in other circumstances.

In the town of Cholet, for example, a falconer ("fauconnier") is employed to help keep at least some of the 10,000 starlings from attempting to

Although most commonly thought of as a rural pursuit, the falconer's skills are in increasing demand in urban situations.

roost in and around the city's ancient buildings. Likewise, the municipality of Perpignan in the Pyrenees have since last year, recruited the services of three falconers in order to help combat the influx of around a million starlings that migrate through the area every autumn.

Other towns utilize the combination of hawk and falconer to deter corvids and seagulls from feeding at refuse dumps and land infill sites, whilst private companies willingly pay to have hawks regularly flown around industrial sites and grain silos that would otherwise be overrun by feral pigeons.

Around the port of Dieppe, seagulls are a particular nuisance, having left their traditional nesting sites on the cliffs in order to set up home in the centre of town. Due to some lateral thinking on the part of the local mayor and commune colleagues, a falconer is now employed two days a week for seven weeks prior to and during the seagull's nesting and breeding season. Continually frightening and harassing the gulls throughout this time makes it virtually impossible for them to lay and hatch off a brood of chicks.

Black is beautiful
29th August 2012

It looks as if, amongst the usual-coloured pheasants, the local shooting club has released several of the melanistic type in readiness for the start of the season in a couple of week's time. I came to this conclusion yesterday when walking at first light, the dog dived into cover and out burst a dozen or more fully grown specimens – far too many for it to have been a wild brood which had managed, against all odds, to reach maturity. Not having seen Maurice or indeed, anyone else connected to the chasse that frequent our area every Sunday morning during the season, I've been unable to find out what the reasoning was behind their decision.

It may, of course, have been something as simple as the fact that melanistics were all that the game farmer had available, or that they were surplus to requirements and therefore much cheaper. It could, though, have been the fact that many shooting people have long considered such birds to fly better and more strongly than some other types of pheasant. Whether they do or not is open to conjecture: they are, however, considered to be a bit of a headache in the opinion of some gamekeepers who cite the fact that they tend to wander more. Personally, I doubt whether they do – it's just that they (like a white "marker" bird) stand out on a stubble field or up a hedgerow and are more noticeable at a quick glance.

Experience tells me that, along with any other minority colours reared in a shed of otherwise "normal" pheasants, melanistics do tend to get picked on due to the fact that the white immature feather tips seen in a young chick or poult are something of a curiosity to the others who peck at them out of inquisitiveness – which can, in turn, cause an out-break of full-blown feather pecking and might require birds to be bitted earlier than would otherwise be the case.

There are other birds and animals known to have melanistic colouring – fallow deer, for example. Occasionally, melanistic grey squirrels might be seen, but not here in France where there are no greys (except perhaps in isolated pockets as a result of them entering over one of the land borders) and we are fortunate in only ever seeing the red variety around our home here at "Le Malineau".

Even then, there can be mistakes in identification and, despite their name, red squirrels vary in colour from the bright chestnut brown typically depicted in children's books, right through to a very dark brown (almost black). Their colour also depends on whether you see them in the winter or the summer: as with all animals, their summer coat obviously being much lighter than the winter one. Interestingly, a photo in a recent issue of the

The odd melanistic pheasant is not uncommon – a whole release pen full is slightly more so!

French monthly magazine, *Le Chasseur Français*, showed a red squirrel, the fur of which was white from the middle of its back and down its haunches, while its tail, shoulders and head parts (apart from a white "moustache") were of the usual russet/red colour.

Hare today, gone tomorrow?
19th March 2014

A morning's walk with the dog always takes half an hour longer than it should at this time of year as there's always so much to look at – not least the ditches in search of wild flowers. Call me an "anorak" if you like but I do often take with me my pocket book of wild flowers. Thank goodness for the "Linnaeus System" as I can check up the names of the flowers in English, find their Latin name in the back of the book and then, upon returning home, check the Latin name against the common one in a French language book of wild flowers. It might seem a long-winded way of going about things and I'll never remember the Latin, but at least it gives me the chance to find out their common names in both English and French – the latter knowledge of which is always useful when talking to Maurice and other neighbours.

Unlike England, where the sight and sound of a skylark is nowadays a rare occurrence, here in our part of France, they are still plentiful and I find it fascinating, although time-consuming, to watch as they climb skywards singing heartily and then "fall" silently and stone-like, back to earth. Not only does watching their antics take up time, it also tends to result in a bad neck as one endeavours to watch their ascent into the heavens. As a schoolboy in Yorkshire, I found the best way was to lie on my back but if I tried doing that on a morning walk nowadays, I would be jumped on by Fideline and my clothes covered in whatever substance she has just discovered in the nearest ditch.

Like skylarks, the hare population in the area immediately surrounding "Le Malineau" is definitely healthy and it would be a rare morning walk not to see at least one but elsewhere in France, it seems that hares suffer mixed fortunes; in some parts they are as plentiful as in the fields around us whilst in others, they are so scarce that the local prefecture will impose a ban on them being shot during the game shooting season.

For such a clean-living and, to my mind, most beautiful animal, it seems incredible that hares are, apparently, quite capable of carrying a number of diseases and here in France, these have included a type of coccidiosis and also tularaemia, which can apparently be transmitted amongst hares by either ticks or mosquitoes.

A decade or so ago, hares were so scarce in Northern France that the relevant shooting associations imported new stock from Poland. Unfortunately, their introduction coincided with several outbreaks of brucellosis (which had at one time been eradicated in France) amongst outdoor breeding herds of pigs and it was thought that it was the hares which were carrying the disease and thus infecting the pigs. Although the pig farmers seemed sure as to the source, I cannot believe that the return of brucellosis was entirely due to the infected hares. Wild boar are also known to be carriers of the disease and, as there are certainly plenty of those around throughout France, I wonder why some of the blame was not laid at their door?

It's easy to waste a lot of time in spring flower identification whilst out on a walk!

Birds of a feather
16th April 2014

Whenever I'm bored at the desk – which happens far more frequently than it should – I enjoy following the most recent travelling done by the migratory woodcock being tracked by the Game and Wildlife Conservation Trust (GWCT). It's all fascinating stuff and its well worth spending any time looking at the relevant website pages (*www.woodcockwatch.com*) whether you're bored or not.

The whole subject of migratory birds of any description is mind-blowing. Not only is it the distances covered by some, but also the sheer stamina necessary to achieve it. What marvellous inbuilt mechanisms they must have to know when it's time to start building up sufficient energy reserves by some intensive eating in order to lay down sufficient amounts of subcutaneous fat to see them through the journey.

Much of what they do is, so I'm led to understand, down to two rhythms: the Circadian, which corresponds to the 24-hour cycle of the earth's rotation, and the Circannual, which corresponds to the annual cycle of the earth's orbit round the sun. Whilst the former dictates daily changes in metabolic rate, body temperature and level of alertness, the latter controls the bird's behavioural pattern and tells it when its time to moult, reproduce and, in the case of migrants, when its time to be on the wing. However, perhaps the most important seasonal indicator to any bird whether it is of the game or garden variety, is by the amount of daylight hours in a given day. Known as "Zeitgebers" (from the German for "time-givers"), they are the reason that a songbird's dawn chorus is greatest in the spring, how a cock pheasant knows that its breeding time, when a partridge begins to nest (at a time when there is likely to be an optimum number of insects on which its chicks can feed) and how the cuckoo knows when to travel.

What is even more special about the cuckoo is that it must all be done entirely by instinct. As they lay their eggs in other bird's nests, they can have no guidance from any older, previously experienced family members when they fly south. The adults (their biological parents) generally leave around July but the young don't leave Europe until a month or so later. At this time of year, they have of course, only just made their way from Africa and their south-east Asian winter grounds. It is possible to almost literally set my clock by the arrival of the first cuckoo around "Le Malineau". Whilst the earliest I've ever heard one here is March 17, it is more usual to hear it between the 21st and 23rd of the month. They seem to have preferred areas too: I can, for instance, go to a particular wood some kilometres away and know I'll hear a cuckoo there at least two days ahead of when I hear one in the wood immediately by the side of the house.

Evolution over millennia has developed a very successful end product when it comes to birds! A pheasant or partridge beak is designed for pulling at vegetation and pecking around for grubs, on-ground seeds and grain; it is, therefore, relatively thick-set and fairly robust – more like a berry-picking finch than a probing long-beaked insect-seeking woodcock. Technically, the beak is split into what are known as the upper and lower mandible and the mouth part, of course, contains no teeth – instead food is passed directly to the crop and subsequently into the gizzard whose rough interior will, with the aid of grit, grind down the food into a sort of paste, the nutrients from which can then be used by the birds' system.

More or less all-round vision is vital to both game birds and songbirds as they need to be constantly on the look out for potential predators as well as food: for the eyes to be set into the side of the head rather than at the front where vision would be limited is, therefore, the obvious solution!

The most distinctive feature of a cock pheasant at this time of year are his wattles. Whilst they are particularly red and prominent about now and must consequently be assumed to have much to do with attracting females, another reason for their existence is that they act as a cooling system because, like a dog (which uses its panting tongue to lose heat), birds cannot sweat, so cool themselves by circulating blood through the wattles and thereby dissipating body heat.

Feathers provide both insulation and waterproofing. The colour of a feather to some extent affects its resilience; for example, black feathers are thought to be more resilient to wear and tear than white ones because they contain more pigmentation. The main pigments are melanin's (manufactured in the bird's body) and carotenoids (which are absorbed from foods, especially greenstuffs and roots). The snow goose, although white, has black tips to its wings due to a high concentration of melanin at this point as this helps strengthen the primary feathers, making them more resilient and capable of the arduous seasonal migrations being undertaken.

The wing feathers of any bird are split into what are known as "primary" and "secondary" (the large ones that can easily be seen along the outer edge) which developed in such a way as to make flight possible. Some of the more gaudy feathers on male birds such as a cock pheasant are designed to attract the opposite sex but, in the case of a pheasant's neck hackles, they are also intended to make the cock look far more aggressive towards any possible threat to his harem. It is not only the obvious contenders that might face a sparring cock bird with his hackles raised; some keepers will, no doubt, have suffered at some time or another as a result of a particular male bird who insists on flying at the back of your legs, hackles set in a ruff formation and spurs ready to do the maximum amount of damage!

8

Books and Things!

E have a large house here in France. I state that not as a
proud boast; more a thankful explanation of the fact that
there's room to store and enjoy some sporting memorabilia
given, bought, collected and misappropriated over the years. I've never had
the inclination or, for that matter, the money to indulge very much in
whatever takes my fancy and so, despite being full of sporting artifacts, "Le
Malineau" is home to either practical or visually pleasurable items rather
than unused gimmicks and products that seemed like a good idea at the
time. Where I fail, however, is in the fact that sporting memories force me
to keep everything and despite knowing that much which surrounds me
will never again serve any useful purpose, it is impossible for me to part
with anything. Very little is valuable as such, but to me it's priceless and far
more evocative than a photograph album.

Various drawers in the house turn out collars, leads and a leather terrier
coupling – all of which remind me of various dogs owned and loved
throughout the years. In the same drawers lie innumerable hip-flasks of
many shapes and sizes, the contents of which I've shared with hunting
folk, Guns and beaters throughout almost the whole of Britain and, in
the latter years, a certain amount of France. In a corner of a drawer which
should only contain kitchen equipment, I've recently discovered a pair of
snap-caps. Momentarily, I couldn't think where they'd come from, but I
quickly remembered that, just as a place to keep them, I'd slipped them

into my tweed jacket pocket whilst loading for a Gun and forgot to replace them at the end of the day!

Every country person's home is littered with bygone traps – isn't it? Our hearth contains a varied selection; none of which are legal, but all of which have been acquired from the dark recesses of various gamekeeper's sheds in Yorkshire, Hampshire, Surrey and Sussex. Illegal though they may be to use, when our redoubtable neighbor Maurice and his ilk pop in to see us, they are a very definite focus of sporting conversation.

Although not directly sporting-orientated, on a shelf, in pride of place, stands a magnificent carved wooden bull. It came into my possession as a result of a very drunken evening at a friend's home when, due shooting in the morning, he suddenly realized that he had no cartridges. I had plenty at my house and so a trade was made – his bull for 250 cartridges. I had the better end of the deal because he fired the cartridges and I still have the pleasure of looking at the bull.

Next to the bull stands a pure silver English partridge given to me by one of the Guns when I left my gamekeeping job in West Sussex – it's

The bull that was swapped for a couple of boxes of cartridges!

weight, and the fact it was made by a prominent London jeweller most famous for be-decking the likes of Elton John and the Beckhams' place it as being extremely high value, but the personal spirit with which it was given makes it priceless.

BOOKS OF THE PAST

I love old books – particularly those to do with hunting and shooting and I'll even read those written by those who would have our chosen sports banned! In December 2007, I happened to be in a second-hand bookshop indulging my passion when I came across a copy of *After Their Blood*, which was published in 1966 and was written by Leslie Pine.

Pine was, in the period between 1960 and 1964, the managing editor of *The Shooting Times*. During this editorship, he apparently traveled all over Britain in connection with his employment and, during that time, experienced most forms of field sports, in the process getting to know many keepers, hunt staff, followers and supporters. The jacket blurb tells the reader that he began his tenure at the Shooting Times desk with "an unbiased attitude [but] he gradually came round to a critical viewpoint"and, as a result of the knowledge acquired during this period, Pine apparently felt he had no option but to resign from his editorial appointment.

In actual fact, it appears that those who knew him believed him to be already "anti" and thought him to have been using his employment as a means of obtaining information which he hoped would support his pre-conceived opinions and could eventually be used to denigrate all kinds of field sports.

The book makes an interesting read but, unfortunately, it is full of wild inaccuracies, particularly when it comes to the management of game shooting. It is, as we are so often told, a free country and, quite rightly, everyone is entitled to their own opinions – they should, however, be based on fact and not, as seems to be the case of *After Their Blood*, as a result of preconceived bias.

Larger than life
28th November 2012

It's physically impossible for me to pass an old-fashioned second-hand bookshop without entering – and I cannot enter such a place without finding something I just have to buy! We were in Tonbridge Wells not all that long ago when I came across a bookshop of the best and most traditional kind and, after perusing the shelves for a fair while, I eventually came away with volumes one and two of *Fifty Years of My Life* by Sir John Dugdale Astley. Published in 1894, my copies have the bonus of being number 541 of a limited edition print run of 880 and the fly leaf of the first volume is inscribed by the author.

Sir John lived from 1828 to 1894 and the two volumes were published just a few months before his death in October of that year. By profession a soldier, it seems that in marrying Eleanor Blanche Mary Corbett, of Elsham Hall, her heiress status ensured that he was thus able to indulge his field sports passions, not least of which was horse racing and betting where he was known for winning and losing large sums of money. In 1867, money was short and Sir John owed a man named Padwick £3,000 – which must have been an incredible figure in those days (a coachman, for example earned just over £50 per annum) so he decided to sell his racehorse "Ostregor" for that amount. When the horse raced in the Chesterfield Cup at Goodwood, Astley backed it to win, which it did by five lengths and in the process, won his old owner £5,000.

Mind you, it appears that he was not alone in his spendthrift attitude and his wife was a willing accomplice in his sporting life. As Sir John writes, "… both self and wife were fond of seeing life, and, not averse to a turn at the tables or a peep at the board of green cloth, we decided a trip to Baden Baden would be a nice change for us; so, leaving the turtle doves, or two young Astleys, under the supervision of their grandpapa, who was highly honoured by the confidence we reposed in him, we started in August, soon after the expiration of the Sussex fortnight."

As far as shooting was concerned, Sir John Dugdale Astley's first introduction to the moors "was as a lad of 16, when, armed with a single-barrelled gun, and one pointer, I killed 19 brace of grouse in Kincardineshire." In later years when times were hard financially, he still managed several days due mainly to the generosity of his friends. Even so he bemoaned the expense saying, "To a man of slender income four days of heavy shooting means, at least, the extermination of a tenner, and more often two tenners by the time you get home."

Always with an eye for the main chance, Sir John never missed the opportunity to benefit from someone else's misfortune when it came to saving money. Take, for instance, the following account: "At Easton one year I fired away 1500 cartridges in the first two days; fortunately for me, one of the party went wrong, as his head could not stand the heavy shooting ... I gently hinted that it might not be worth his while to lug his remaining cartridges up to London, and, like a real good fellow, he bid his servant hand them over to my loader."

Sir John was also fond of any sort of hound-work; especially coursing and hunting. Of particular personal interest because of the fact I know the area well and have hunted with the Hampshire Hunt myself in the past, is Astley's account of when, in 1849, his battalion was moved to Chichester and he had several days' hunting with the same pack. They were then apparently hunted by "Gentleman Smith" – a rare old warrior who was said to know the line of every fox in his country. Assuming that the Duke of Richmond would have had hounds at Goodwood, I was surprised to read that, according to Sir John, "There were no hounds at Goodwood at that time, or for some years afterwards." Subsequent research shows that the Duke of Richmond's original pack was disbanded in 1813 (the kennels for which were adapted as accommodation for staff – and are now home to an incredibly up-market restaurant!). New kennels were, however, begun in 1882 when the 6th Duke decided to create the Goodwood Hunt and these buildings can still be seen today.

Other aspects of Sir John Dugdale Astley's sporting life included stalking, live pigeon shooting from traps and cock fighting; both before and after it was banned in 1847. How the account of this man's extraordinary life all came to be written was seemingly as a result of his constant need for money and a lunch with friends in Grosvenor Place, London. After regaling them with his tales, one apparently was moved to remark; "Why don't you write a book? You are constantly complaining of poverty, why you would be a rich man, if you would take the trouble to put pen to paper." To which Sir John responded by declaring, "It's all very well, my dear Charlie, to talk. Any fool can tell a story, but it takes a man to write a book."

Man or not, the two volumes of *Fifty Years of My Life* were eventually written and published and are a fascinating, sometimes unbelievable

Sir John Astley had a sporting life of which most of us can only dream!

account of how life was lived amongst the upper echelons of Victorian high society – as well as being a far more useful record of British social history than any number of episodes of television's Downton Abbey!

Be prepared!
20th December 2006

If, like me, you were a Cub and a Scout; a Brownie and a Guide, or are a military historian, then the name of Lord Robert Baden-Powell will be familiar to you either as the founder of the Scouting organisation; the husband of the founder of Guiding, or as the saviour of Mafeking during the Boar War. Although well-known for creating the internationally popular youth movement and for his military prowess, he is perhaps less so for his interest in field sports – all varieties of which he enjoyed, no matter where in the world he happened to find himself.

In *Lessons from the Varsity of Life*, published in 1933 and written when he was 76 years old, Baden-Powell writes interestingly and amusingly of his exploits while shooting, fishing, hunting and playing polo. Although long ago out of print, but perhaps still available through the Internet, I include four quite startling quotes of his experiences here. If nothing else, it seems the man had a sense of humour and occasion!

170

Woodcock shooting in Albania

"Someone said only yesterday, talking of shooting, 'woodcock shooting is the most dangerous sport in the world.' Well it is fairly risky when you are covert shooting in England and the beggar flies low, dodging hither and thither, and every single gun within sight of him risks a shot. But in its own country, say Albania, where it is not a rarity, you shoot more calmly, more carefully, and with better effect.

That was a ripping country to shoot in. It's getting too civilised now, but a few years ago, when I went there in a yacht (the only way of getting there); we anchored in a perfect land-locked little bay and went ashore every day for shooting.

The law there was that you had to take a soldier with you as escort. His payment was sixpence a day, and unlimited cigarettes. Then you got a few villagers and their dogs to come with you as beaters.

They were a picturesque-looking lot of ruffians and naturally so because their other role was that of brigands, by whom you would be trapped and hauled off to be ransomed, unless you were under Government protection, as evidenced by your soldier escort. But in their capacity as beaters they were excellent fellows, hard and cheesy blackguards and good sportsmen.

The dogs of that country were a special feature in the picture. They were trained to attack strangers, the idea being to prevent the stealing of sheep. If one saw a flock of sheep grazing on the hill-side one kept very wide of it because each flock was guarded by three or four dogs. These beggars would lie around while the sheep grazed, but if a strange man appeared on the scene the nearest dog would go for him, calling up the others to the attack, and they would not be happy until they pulled him down.

There was a strict law against shooting a dog even in self-defence, and it imposed very heavy penalties for doing so, but you were allowed to stab him if he got so near as to be within your reach.

A very well-known sportsman, hailing from Essex, who had been shooting in Albania, told me that he had suffered an attack from one of these dogs, and in self-defence he shot him. Then remembering the law he promptly set to work to bury the dog before anyone should see him.

Just as he was in the middle of this operation the owner of the dog came upon him. 'My goodness!' I said: 'What did you do then?'

'Oh, there was nothing else for it. I buried him too.'"

Quail shooting in South Africa

"I had a dear old Boer friend in South Africa who, when he was harvesting his corn, left narrow strips of it standing which the quail came to use as cover. They were thus easily walked up. On the first day that I shot over his ground he accompanied me in his Cape cart, with refreshments.

When I shot my first quail he shouted out his admiration, but when shortly afterwards I got a right and left and bagged them both his enthusiasm was unbounded. He said he had never seen anything like this before and it was a matter for celebration; so accordingly the stone bottle of brandy was uncorked and libation offered.

He then examined my gun with great curiosity and wonder. It turned out that he had never seen a shot-gun and had supposed all the time that I was shooting those tiny birds with a rifle!"

Pheasant shooting in England

"I never went in for making big bags of game. As a rule I only shot for the pot excepting, of course, when out covert shooting in England. Here on one occasion I beat all records.

My pick up at one stand alone was something like fifty birds when I had only fired twenty cartridges. My host had engaged the services of the local Boy Scouts to act as beaters and he stationed one Scout behind each gun to mark down and collect the birds he shot. At the end of the beat, when I turned to leave my stand, I found this pile of birds to my credit. I then realised that behind the line of guns the boys had surreptitiously passed along some of the birds shot by the other men as contributions to my heap! Such is esprit de corps among the Boy Scouts!"

Fox-hunting

"Fox-hunting, when you come to think of it, is really a very wonderful institution. Although it has come to be quite an artificial sport in a wholly civilised country it still keeps going in every part of England in spite of the War, in spite of the decline in horse-breeding, and in spite of heavy taxes and heavier costs. It is one of the few old institutions left which still keeps us in touch today with the traditions and spirit of the former Old England."

A PICTURE PAINTS 1,000 WORDS

Both my wife and I like paintings on the wall and the house is full of ones that we've acquired both separately and together. My own collection depicting hunting, shooting and fishing sits, sometimes at odds, amongst hers but nonetheless, each has a tale to tell and they were either given as gifts, or bought in the past when the end-of-season tips accrued during my life as a gamekeeper meant that a "little treat" was in order.

Generally, though, sporting art has always been popular – and originals from the likes of Munnings, Herring and Alken, expensive to purchase as a consequence. Prints are, however, mercifully cheap and it is perhaps no accident that many aesthetically pleasing prints are of a typical book size as, during the 1960s and 1970s, it was the fashion for second-hand book sellers to buy up cartons-full of unwanted sporting tomes originally published in the early part of the century and then cut out and frame some of the best illustrations for onward sale. Sacrilege to the 21st Century sportsman and woman, the practice did at least ensure that the finest examples of art remain for our enjoyment and, in some cases, it may be a legitimate way of saving illustrations when other parts of the book had been irreparably damaged.

Buy it if you like it
8th July 2009

The French are quite fond of sporting prints. As with the UK, any country shows being held here at this time of year generally have a couple of stands on which sporting prints are displayed for purchase. Unlike the UK, though, much of what is on show can best be described as rubbish and has obviously spent the past decade or so in the back of someone's loft, causing dampness and "foxing" to affect both the picture and its mount. Having said that, last weekend at a "fête de chasse et peche", I did buy a very clean and almost pristine looking picture of an otter hunt painted onto silk. It shows two members of hunt staff in uniform, one of whom is holding an otter above his head by means of a small pitchfork type affair whilst the other is standing in the water holding back a couple of hounds. It is not, I must admit, the prettiest of paintings but as a social record of how hunting used to be carried out, I thought it well worth buying.

Sporting prints are fascinating because there are so many varieties of subject and size, and so many ways of producing them. Often they are of the type known as "aquatints", which are in fact a combination of etching and aquatint – where etching is used for the outlines and aquatint solution for the tones. The most common form of aquatinting involved the use of a resin dissolved in spirit which was then poured over the surface of a warmed etching plate (generally made of copper), onto which had been applied a layer of wax and into which the etcher had drawn the picture's outline with the point of a sharp needle. As the spirit evaporated, it left tiny granules of resin on the surface. After being printed onto special paper – that most usually used being produced by Whatman – the picture would then be hand finished with watercolours.

Many of the framed and mounted pictures of bye-gone sporting life that you may see as you walk around the shows during the summer months are likely to have been taken from books published during the first three decades of last century and showcase the work of brilliant sporting artists such as Lucy Kemp-Welsh, Cecil Aldrin, F.A. Stewart, G.D. Armour,

An illustration of otter hunting – acquired at a local "vide-grenier".

Lionel Edwards, Cuthbert Bradley and of course, Charles Johnson-Payne, a.k.a. "Snaffles" who is, I think, my all-time favourite. Ironically, back in 1972, I had the opportunity to buy seven of his limited edition prints and one original painting for the sum total of what just one of his prints would be likely to cost now. Not doing so is one of my few regrets, as, not only would I have had the great pleasure of looking at them for the past 37 years; in retrospect, they would have proved a far better investment than money in the bank.

PRECIOUS POCKET KNIVES

There is, in the village of Barret, situated in the Charente area of France, a modern-day pocket-knife maker whose various designs are real works of art. Pascal Renoux is the son-in-law of the village blacksmith and began his craft at the forge before eventually moving to a workshop on the outskirts of the village from where he now runs a business co-owned by himself and Jean-Marc Debai. Not only do the two of them make new knives, they also restore them. Originally though, Pascal was more interested in creating and restoring suits of armour and medieval swords (apparently it can take two craftsmen twelve months to manufacture a full suit of armour) and it was not until setting up business together in 2001 that knives became the main product.

Their company, "Coutellerie d'Art Renoux" makes custom-built knives as well as pocket knives. All made to Pascal's own design, the handles can be made of horn, bone or wood. Always environmentally conscious, any wood used is either sourced locally or, where an exotic wood is required, salvaged from boat-yards and cabinet-makers. Handles might also be adorned with gold or silver decorations, but it is the blade of some that is the most fascinating because they are forged in such a way as to form the "Damascus" pattern or design seen on the barrels of old shotguns. The result is achieved by a process of working both white and black steel together.

Many of the knives, whilst designed by Pascal, are based on traditional items known in the region for generations. The "Charente", for example, can be used both as a table tool and a general purpose pocket knife, while the "St Jacques" model is similar to one used by pilgrims and is made in

A selection of pocket knives – from some of the best French artisans.

such a way that it can be opened single-handed, a very useful attribute in so many countryside and field sports situations. However, possibly the most intriguing knife made by Coutellerie d'Art Renoux is their "Couteaux à Secret" which closely follows an idea popular in the 1700s whereby every knife of its type has a slightly different mechanism for opening the blade, and which is only ever shown to the purchaser. They are not cheap though: prices for this particular model (without any engraving) are in the region of 1,200 euros. Other types are perhaps a little more affordable and a pocket knife can be yours from 120 euros, whilst their custom-built knives begin at 600 euros. Definitely not an item to be lost or mislaid!

Lost in France
7th May 2008

I've lost yet another pocket knife. Quite how or where, I have no idea, but the fact remains that the latest loss is just another in a long line of many. When working in the UK, it was an easy matter to cut the strings of straw bales out on the feed rides or on a bale of hay for my horse and then leave the knife stuck in a fence post, tree trunk or in another bale. On other occasions, I'd stick the knife in my shirt or waistcoat pocket and lose it bending over to pick up a bag of feed or top up a water trough. By the time I'd realized it had gone, I'd invariably forget where I'd last used it and, despite much wandering up and down in all the likely places, hardly ever managed to find it.

Still, if nothing else, it made the problem of birthday and Christmas presents easier for my family and friends and it was always a safe bet if they chose to buy me a knife. At first they would choose a replacement with great care and even go to the trouble of having it embellished with my initials or other form of personalization, but as the years wore on, they realized such attention to detail was a waste of time, as their gift would most likely be lost within months, if not weeks.

My most recent lock-knife is probably the oldest I've ever had and its easy familiarity means that I shall grieve its loss even more than usual. The reason for its longevity is probably because I nowadays have less cause to use a pocket knife, unlike the old gamekeeping times when it would be in constant use. Apart from cutting the odd piece of string with which to tie up a brace of birds or a piece of rose bush in the garden, the only other use it ever got these days was to sharpen a pencil – admittedly not much of a job for a "macho" tool.

Of course, no sportsman should be without a knife of some description, but in Britain the law restricts what one can legally carry during the course of general day-to-day activities. I think I'm right in saying that, unless you have a good reason, i.e. you're a fisherman who is at the time fishing, you can only carry a pocket knife that is non-locking and has a blade length of less than two and a half inches. There are no such restrictions here in France, a fact which will make my eventual choice of a replacement knife so much easier.

I am seriously considering the purchase of a Laguiole (pronounced "ley-ole") knife. After all, when in France, do as the French do! As I understand it, despite it initially being given to a specific type of knife that has its origins in a small town of the same name situated in the Aveyron region of France, the name "Laguiole" is generic. Originally, though, this particular style of knife was a non-locking version of locking knives brought back from Spain by French workers who would travel over the border in search of seasonal employment. The blade was long and curved slightly upwards and the handles constructed wide from side-to-side and could be made of bone, antler, ivory or wood.

Since those early beginnings, it is probably no exaggeration to say that millions of these knives have been made by countless knife makers and, although it is no longer necessary for them to be made in the town of Laguiole, they must however, be of French manufacture. Despite the name not being patented, the shape and style of the knife does have to conform to certain criteria: for example, the length of the blade should be wider than the width of your palm; the back-spring forged in one piece and, on the more expensive types, hand-filing or "guillochage", is evident on the back-spring and spine of the blade. Traditionally, a Laguiole knife should also feature the emblem of a bee and a cross of inlaid metal pins.

With the French enthusiasm for knives of all kinds, it should be a simple matter to find exactly what I'm looking for in a local gun-shop or at one of the summer "fêtes de la chasse", but if I do have any difficulties, it might be worthwhile making a trip down to the Dordogne and buying one at the "Festival of Knives", which is held at Nontron each August.

This annual event is basically a showcase for many of the well-known knife-makers of France and, unlike in the UK where displays of knives would be kept in locked glass-fronted cabinets; at Nontron, there is no outward evidence of any security measures: as a consequence, it is possible to pick up and examine any knife that takes your fancy. And be sure that at least one of them will, for in this little Aladdin's Cave of the cutler's art, there are some of the best examples of hunting, skinning, kitchen and pocket knives to be found anywhere in the country.

Craftsmen in the village have been making a particular type of pocket knife for over 500 years and even today, each knife made is an individual piece created by one of only half a dozen artisans. Like the Laguiole, a "Nontron" has some unique trade-mark features, the most notable of which is that each boxwood handle is decorated with a mysterious-looking symbol. In years gone by, the acquisition of such a knife was considered a rite of passage from boyhood into maturity – it's a good job no-one ever considered giving one to me on the occasion of my 18th birthday as I would undoubtedly have lost it well before the party had ended!

SPORTING INCIDENTALS

As well as books and things, the odd stuffed animal, trophy or fish adorns the study of many a fieldsports man and woman. Some notes on how to clean a dead animal might, therefore be in order – but before I offer them, I feel that I should perhaps begin this particular piece with a disclaimer! Christophe Barbarin is a French taxidermist of note and recently offered some simple ideas on how to keep mounted wall trophies clean and, as he says, "comme neuf" (like new) using only regular household products. I was fascinated by his ideas and thought them well worth passing on. They are, however, included on the strict understanding that I take no responsibility for anyone trying them out on their 100-year plus family heirlooms!

Firstly, and quite safely, I would have thought, Christophe suggests cleaning the antlers and the wooden shield on which the head is mounted by the simple expedient of wiping the surfaces with a damp cloth and then, if the wood is dull in appearance after years of neglect, to softly wipe it with a cloth, onto which has been applied a light mixture of turpentine and linseed oil. Finally, both shield and antlers should be sprayed and dusted with a clean cloth.

For the eyes, a little more care might be needed as, whilst Christophe's recommendation is to clean the main glass part with a little window cleaner applied with the aid of a cotton-bud, he does warn against not touching the outer parts of the eye as certain chemicals contained in some cleaners can be quite aggressive and may possibly damage the skin into which the taxidermist has fitted the glass. Protect these areas further by holding a piece of kitchen paper against them.

In modern houses, the skin of the animal's nose can dry out over time. Christophe's way of remedying such a problem is to place a couple of damp tissues over it and leave them for several hours in the hope that by doing so, the skin will re-hydrate. Any visible cracking of the skin can be carefully filled with filler paste, after which it should be painted with black shoe polish, applied with a tiny brush.

If your trophy is really bad and, as Christophe puts it, "resembles the décor normally seen on the set of a horror film", he suggests that you clean the fur of dust and spiders' webs by either wiping it with a damp cloth or one which has been soaked with "denatured" (presumably pure

Keeping a selection of mounted heads clean can prove a daunting task!

– and definitely not the sort to drink!) alcohol diluted in a little water. Christophe stresses that it is important to only wipe the fur in the way in which it lies naturally and never in the opposite direction.

Hip flask envy
17th December 2008

In the days when I used to hunt regularly, as well as the main purpose of watching hounds work and being able to ride over land not normally accessible whilst out on a hack, part of the pleasure was, during quiet moments, to share conversation and the contents of a hip flask. I always wanted to own a saddle flask, but couldn't afford to buy one of these magnificent glass-constructed, silver-topped, leather-holstered and, to my mind, absolutely essential pieces of hunting equipment. Despite huge hints, "Father Christmas" never obliged and, as often as I went, I was never fortunate enough to find a second-hand one cheap enough at sporting auctions. So it was that, when everyone else un-strapped their liquid refreshment during a convenient pause in the proceedings, I had to reach into my jacket pocket and, rather shame-faced, hand around the hip flask I normally used for shooting days.

There are those who might say that it is what's in the flask rather than the flask itself that matters, but, rather like drinking good quality wine out of a plastic cup, it just doesn't taste the same to me unless it is drunk from an appropriate receptacle.

Hip flasks are many and varied. There's a particular shooting man infamous throughout the southern counties for his huge pewter affair that must hold two or three bottles of liqueur – filling it must be a bit like putting petrol into the tanks of a Rolls-Royce. Still, his flask is in keeping with his larger-than-life character: big man, big flask.

The majority, though, are more conventional in size and shape and have been around in this form since the 1700s. Some of the earliest, particularly those made of silver, are now much sought-after collector's items, but to be of any real value, they must be in pristine condition. Personally, I prefer mine to have a few dents and a story to tell. It would, for instance, be quite fun to own a hip flask that originated from 1920s America when the

Hip flasks of a moderate – and more usual size!

Prohibition Act meant that they were a popular way of transporting and secreting illegal alcohol. In fact, along with cocktail shakers, hip flasks were banned. More fun still to acquire one previously owned by an American lady of the time, as they were quite often kept in their garter for safe-keeping.

With or without provenance, a hip-flask (although often stowed in a jacket pocket) should, by tradition be kept in your shooting breeches and should rest just below your hip joint … and never below your knee! If, as a Gun once asked his wife, "does this flask make me look fat?" I think it's pretty safe to assume that it's larger than it should be!

Somewhere to sit
21st October 2009

Not all that long ago, my wife and I were in the French town of Nantes and came across an antique shop. In such places I always look for paintings, bronze sculptures and anything field sports related. Most are priced unrealistically but occasionally there are bargains to be had.

Outside this particular establishment, and well amongst the rubbish, was a very old, but extremely serviceable three-legged shooting stick with a leather seat and complete with a carrying strap. The price was only 15 euros. Being a fan of any piece of sporting equipment that might have a history and imagining it as perhaps having been sat on regularly by some big-bottomed well-to-do French Count, I offered 10 euros for its historic interest, but the proprietor was not prepared to negotiate any sort of deal. Despite it being good value, I had no real use for it and left it where it was. Had I have realised that brand new in France, a similar thing would have cost 70 euros and in England, considerably more, I might well have been tempted.

I'm never sure about the true value of a shooting seat. It seems from my experience that Guns tend to perhaps use them for the first few minutes whilst waiting for a drive to begin and then they are just abandoned in all the excitement. They often get in the way of the Gun and loader once the birds start coming over and are frequently forgotten about at the end of the drive; necessitating a return trip to the peg at lunchtime in order to retrieve the offending article.

Wicker and willow
25th June 2014

A friend of mine has just bought herself an old wicker fishing creel from a local vide-grenier and I'm quite envious – especially as she only paid seven euros for it! I don't frequent such places very often but when I do, I'm always on the look-out for any sporting items made of leather or wicker which look like they may have a bit of history to them.

Wicker items have long had a number of uses within the world of field-sports; not least of which are the lunchtime food hampers so often seen at point-to-points and prestigious race meetings such as Royal Ascot. There's something about a traditional hamper that improves a picnic: Charles Dickens wrote of one Epsom Derby: "Look where I will ... I see Fortnum & Mason. All the hampers fly wide open and the green downs burst into a blossom of lobster salad!"

Fortnum & Mason are still very much the name one thinks of when it comes to wicker hampers. Apparently, way back in the mid 1800s, the company led the way in producing ready-to-eat luxury foods such as "poultry and game in aspic, hard-boiled eggs in forcemeat ... boar's heads, truffles, mangoes ... all decorated and prepared so as to require no cutting." Whilst they might not have needed cutting, they did, however, need something in which they could be carried and a wicker hamper seemed to fit the bill very well indeed.

The use of picnic hampers was not confined to the racecourse or any of the other traditional summer season events such as the Henley Regatta and they were (and are still) the perfect receptacle in which to transport lunchtime provisions onto the grouse moor when the August weather was usually kind enough to allow lunch to be partaken outside whilst sitting in the heather. Harold Macmillan was apparently famous for discussing affairs of state over a grouse shooting al-fresco lunch!

Wicker hampers were also useful on the moors as a means of transporting shot grouse back to the game larder. The majority were rectangular and grouse could be packed in such a way that air could circulate through the wicker weaving but the gaps were generally small enough to prevent, or at least deter, access by flies keen to lay their eggs.

On some upland estates, the wicker baskets used to transport grouse down from the hill on the backs of ponies were more of a traditional fishing creel shape and were contoured in such a way as to be attached one either side of the animal. I am sure that these types of baskets will still be in use in the Highlands – and there will probably be many more tucked away un-used in the back of out-buildings and shooting lodges.

Fishing creels and eel traps

The word "creel" has been around a long time – Webster's dictionary says it is a Middle English word and dates from sometime between the years 1250 and 1450. They have not always been made of wicker as, in the late 17th Century, many were made from leather and it was at least a century later before the designs we recognise today began to appear.

In fact it seems that I might be wrong to have described my French friend's newly purchased fishing creel as being wicker as apparently, "wicker" is, strictly speaking, strips of split bamboo – and most fishing creels are made from willow. It makes sense as woven willow will tolerate getting wet periodically and, according to one modern day creel-maker, "willow contains tannin, a natural preservative, which will keep your catch fresh all day."

It appears there are many (like me!) who like the design and history of old creels as, from a quick look on Ebay, whilst there are several vintage or antique ones to choose from, the prices are quite high – particularly in America where it appears collecting such items is a very popular pastime. Like fishing creels, "wicker" eel traps were not made from wicker at all but willow cut from the locality of the river. They are, I think, now mainly seen as rural life museum exhibits and have been replaced on the river with far more long-lasting materials.

Wicker on horseback

In the days when terrier-men were mounted on horse-back, they would often carry their terriers in a leather "satchel" but it was not unknown for them to use a basket similar in appearance to a fishing creel. Some of the old hunting and riding books show very young children (between the ages of six and 18 months) sitting in a wicker basket saddle fitted on the back of a family pony. They were, in essence, very like a small chair with a back and arm rests and, on several designs, there were attached leather toe stirrups – in which a child could gain support but there was no danger of their foot becoming trapped should he or she fall.

The best were padded with horse-hair and all generally had a lap-strap similar to an airplane safety belt. You would be lucky to find one nowadays at either a French vide-grenier or a UK car-boot sale and, if you did, I'm willing to bet you'd have to part with quite a bit of money to buy it! There is, though, at least one manufacturer of equestrian equipment, based in Sussex, who can supply a modern version of this most traditional of riding accoutrements.